MURAL MANUAL

How to paint murals
for the classroom,
community center,
and street corner

MURAL
MANUAL

MARK ROGOVIN
MARIE BURTON
HOLLY HIGHFILL

edited by
Tim Drescher

introduction by
Pete Seeger

Beacon Press
Boston

We dedicate the Mural Manual to Paul
Robeson, Pete Seeger, Pablo Neruda,
Brigada Ramona Para, David Siqueiros,
the Chicago Muralists, and to all other
artists and art organizations whose art has
furthered the struggle for an end to racism,
for peace, justice and human dignity
throughout the world.

Copyright © 1973 by Public Art Workshop

Second edition copyright © 1975 by Public Art Workshop

Beacon Press books are published under the auspices
of the Unitarian Universalist Association

Published simultaneously in hardcover and paperback editions

Library of Congress Cataloging in Publication Data

Rogovin, Mark.
    Mural manual.

    1. Mural painting and decoration--Technique.
2. Community art projects. I. Burton, Marie, joint
author. II. Highfill, Holly, joint author.
III. Title.
ND2550.R63 1975   751.4   74-16670
ISBN 0-8070-6652-4
ISBN 0-8070-6653-2 pbk.

COVER PHOTO IDENTIFICATION

Top left: Detail, "Wall of Brotherhood," Mario
    Castillo, director, Chicago (photo by Harold Allen).
Bottom left: "Against Domestic Colonialism," Arnold
    Belkin, New York.
Right: (photo by Ted Lacey).

Contents

Introduction

Americans are drowned in words -- over the air, in directives on paper, in appeals through the mails.

We're also drowned in pictures -- outdoor advertising, transit advertising, advertising on pages of paper, or in blurry pictures on a little screen.

The independent graphic artist in America has in the past occupied himself or herself with filling rectangles to be hung on interior walls. Usually only a small percentage of people will pay for such art, or even find wall space for it.

Now an increasing number of graphic artists are realizing the need to use exterior surfaces, visible to any pedestrian, cyclist, or to passengers in car, bus, or train. It's an old technique, used by ancient societies in all countries, and today still in some places.

Sometimes it has been a folk art, of anonymous painters filling the people's needs. Sometimes, as in Mexico, the artists have been national heroes.

This manual will help young artists expand the tradition here. Now. In the crisis facing the inhabitants of this land, murals can fill a need for honest communication between all people on a nonverbal level. Independent artists can communicate ideas which will not be said by our politicians, our TV or newspapers -- ideas which need to be explored in public.

Not all the artists will agree with each other, of course. No matter. Their noncommercial pictures will carry an important message: we are not 100 percent at the mercy of the media. We can communicate with each other through color, line, and form. And as independent human beings, our content is going to be different from what is ground out on the drawing boards of commerce: we are going to build a new world. We are going to unite for peace, freedom, jobs for all, and a clean, unpolluted world to share.

How will this come about? The murals will tell the story. You don't believe me?

Keep your eyes open.

Pete Seeger

Pete Seeger
Beacon, New York

Preface

This manual, compiled from our own experience, the experience of friends, and in consultation with technical experts, is the first complete guide to community-based mural painting in recent years. It covers almost all aspects of mural painting. It presents the technical aspects of paints, wall preparation, scaffolding, and insurance. It deals with artistic and practical problems of developing a theme and a sketch, transferring the sketch to the wall, and painting on a large scale for a public audience. It suggests many different types of murals and mural themes. Throughout, the manual contains our own theoretical view of mural painting and of public art. We ourselves are muralists, part of an expanding and vital public art movement. We have written this manual in order to further expand and strengthen the recent renaissance in mural painting.

Since the summer of 1967, there has been a rapidly growing movement involved in the production of large outdoor murals. This renaissance began in Chicago. It received its major impetus from the painting of the "Wall of Respect," a huge and magnificent outdoor mural done under the leadership of William Walker on Chicago's South Side. Having its beginning there, in the black community and under the leadership of black artists, this rebirth in mural painting has grown into a new direction for disenfranchised artists of all communities and a new form to give voice to all people.

The recent mural movement has been made up to a large degree of artists who have determined to reject the goal of "making it" in the galleries and private collections. These artists, including ourselves, have selected instead a new audience for works of art. The priority audience for which we paint is the audience of our own communities, working people of all ethnic backgrounds. Our subject matter comes from the history and culture, the needs and struggles, of communities. Our art speaks of the dignity of the people and projects a vision of a future free from war and exploitation. The form we have chosen is murals. Murals can be a great way of reaching thousands upon thousands of people, since they are in public places, accessible to everyone. They are a wonderful form to educate and inspire.

We know that a manual such as this would have been invaluable to us in working on our first projects. We are sure that at least some of the many subjects covered in the manual will be of help to almost anyone newly involved in mural painting -- from the student, to the classroom teacher, to the community artist. Each mural poses new aesthetic, technical, and social problems, and it is impossible to anticipate all of them. We hope that this manual will anticipate, and answer, many of these questions for you.

One of the trends in the recent mural renaissance is simply to decorate walls with patterns of color.

We see murals as much more than decoration. While murals do add color and liveliness to a neighborhood, this is not our main objective. In our view, those muralists who are most effective use color and form not as an end product, but as tools for conveying a specific subject matter. Further, this subject matter is expressed by means of a public symbolism easily understood by a general audience, rather than in private or personal symbols to be interpreted by only a few. Murals that truly speak for a community and its social concerns are a real inspiration -- both as a model for artists and as a monument to the struggles and aspirations of the community.

The mural can be an important means of helping students learn to work together in the classroom. The classroom mural also gives young people the opportunity to explore and celebrate their own cultural heritage and to further contribute to its development. The murals themselves can be valuable in making the school environment more exciting, in raising issues, and in standing as an example of the talents and accomplishments of the students.

To build a future for public art, we need to seek out new materials, new sponsors, government and local subsidies, new walls. We would like to see serious concern and involvement in public art and murals on the college level. The college could be one valuable training ground for future muralists. Serious study would be done on the history of murals, the muralists and their times, and other related areas. The total school could be involved in experimenting and developing materials for murals. Many departments -- ceramics, painting, environmental design, sculpture, film, photography, etc. -- would lend their expertise. Workshops would involve students in designing murals in conjunction with communities. It would assist students in working with architects and engineers. Students would gain experience in relation to public symbolism, with architectural space, the mobile viewer, and new tools and technology for the muralist and more.

We need to work for full-time employment of artists -- sculptors, painters, actors, musicians, dancers, writers, muralists -- working for the general public. We should work toward the day when new public facilities -- public housing, schools, hospitals, government buildings -- will integrate works of art into their original designs.

In building a strong future for public art, we know that there will have to be a shift of priorities in this society. There will have to be a change from a monstrous military budget as a way of life to an economy whose first priority is serving the needs of the people at home -- building decent housing, schools, child care centers, adequate transportation systems, medical care for all, and more. We feel that artists can be of aid in bringing about such a change in priorities. This is the overriding reason for our commitment to mural painting and we dedicate this manual as a vehicle for you to join in working toward this goal.

All profits received by the authors of the *Mural Manual*, from its sale, will go to the expansion of the nationwide Mural Resource Center of the Public Art Workshop. The Public Art Workshop is a storefront mural workshop and resource center on Chicago's West Side. It has grown out of the recent U.S. mural renaissance. The workshop was formally opened on April 23, 1972. It has been supported largely by the financial contributions and donated services of community residents and others who were convinced of the need for such a center.

We are a group of artists, West Side community residents, and others who see art as a vehicle for bringing about social change. We want to be an influence in the development of a thrust toward public art. We see this as an instrument for political change and the activation of a broader cultural force against the alienation and dehumanization in our society. The workshop both initiates projects and joins with other groups involved in current struggles against racism, exploitation, and repression, and toward peace, justice, and human dignity.

The primary activity of the workshop is the production of indoor and outdoor murals. These mural projects involve staff and other resident community artists. We are developing a new and exciting dimension in the mural movement -- the production of portable murals. Also, we have extended our services to many groups in the production of street theater props. Our program also includes art classes for youths and adults.

In addition to its art production, the Public Art Workshop serves as a resource center to promote public art and functions as a means of communication and encouragement among artists. Slides of Mexican and U.S. murals, a film about murals, slide talks, and mural demonstrations are available through the workshop. We are developing a library of books, magazines, and clippings on murals and other public art forms. We are presently engaged in a research project (with photo documentation) on murals painted in the Chicago area during the 1930s New Deal period.

We hope this manual will serve to further the expansion of the mural movement -- our basic ideas are stated in practice throughout the manual. We are anxious to get responses from our readers. If you have any suggestions of new tools, better techniques, or futher shortcuts or tips, please send them to us. If you find that we have not covered an area about which you have information to share, or if you have any specific questions or further ideas (theoretical or technical), please write to us. We would especially appreciate any news of your projects -- diaries, photos or slides of murals in progress, and so on. We hope you will pass this manual on to friends and other artists.

--The Authors
Public Art Workshop
5623 West Madison Street
Chicago, Illinois 60644

About the Authors

Mark Rogovin:

"Mural work is not a new phenomenon, but today it has an especially powerful function -- being both a vehicle for disenfranchised artists of all communities and a voice for the people. For myself, mural painting was a logical direction to take; it gave me a chance to weld together both my ideology and my artistic skills into a single public expression."

In 1967 and 1968, Mark worked for 5 months as an assistant to the great Mexican muralist David Alfaro Siqueiros on his "March of Humanity" mural. In 1968 he received his BFA degree in painting from the Rhode Island School of Design and continued on at the School of the Art Institute of Chicago to get his MFA degree in 1970. During the years 1971-1973, he taught courses at Columbia College, the School of the Art Institute of Chicago, Elmhurst College, and Rosary College. In 1972 he was one of the founders and is now director of the Public Art Workshop, a mural workshop and nationwide mural resource center on Chicago's West Side.

Mark is one of the leaders in the recent mural upsurge in the U.S. He directed his first mural in 1969 and has since engaged in collective community-based mural projects in over fifteen locations. He has also given numerous slide talks and mural workshops around the U.S.

Marie Burton:

"I love mural painting -- and if this guide to creating murals makes it any more practical and enjoyable for teachers and others, I'll feel happy having written it. With my students, I have found mural work a rich experience -- a way of expressing deep feelings about the stream of human emotions, struggles, and triumphs."

In 1965 Marie received a B.A. degree in fine arts from Mundelein College. In 1966 and 1972 she studied at the School of the Art Institute of Chicago and in 1967 at the College of Art, San Francisco. She is working toward a Master's degree at the University of Wisconsin in Milwaukee. From 1968 to the present she has been the coordinator of the art department and Street Arts Program at St. Mary's Center for Learning, Chicago. Presently she is director of murals for the Milwaukee Youth Foundation.

Marie has directed murals at St. Mary's Center for Learning and the Alliance to End Repression, a children's mural at Marillac House, Chicago, and several murals in Milwaukee.

Holly Highfill:

"I think that mural making is important as a humanizing force. It expresses the value of human feelings and needs and brings this expression into people's daily lives. I do murals because through them I can communicate with other people, not just paint for myself, and this is my reason for painting."

Holly received a B.A. in history of art from Bryn Mawr College in 1969. The following year she attended the Pennsylvania Academy of Fine Arts in Philadelphia, and in 1971-72 worked as a writer and editor in art history for *Encyclopedia Britannica*. In 1973-74 she worked as information director at the Public Art Workshop and is currently employed as a muralist by the Uptown Educational Program in Chicago.

Holly has directed murals for Clergy and Laity Concerned, the Uptown Community Organization, and the Uptown Educational Program, as well as several small murals in the Chicago area.

Acknowledgments

Drafts of both the first and second editions of this manual were sent to muralists around the country. The following artists responded with statements of encouragement, additions, and suggestions to be incorporated into the manual. We at the Public Art Workshop are delighted to have received their help in strengthening this document:

Judy Baca, Venice, California; Arnold Belkin, New York; Lillian Brulc, Joliet, Illinois; Jesus Campusano, San Francisco; Susan Caruso-Green, New York; Leonard Castillanos, East Los Angeles; Mitchell Caton, Chicago; Eva Cockcroft, Highland Park, New Jersey; Mario Galan, Chicago; Jose Gonzalez, Hammond, Indiana; Jim Yanigisawa, Chicago; Kathy Judge, Chicago; Samuel Leyba, Santa Fe; Lucy Mahler, New York; Alan Ocada, New York; Ray Patlan, Chicago; Anton Refregier, Woodstock, New York; Gary Rickson, Boston; Hector Luis Rosario, Chicago; David Torrez, Midland, Michigan; Marie Turley, Somerville, Massachusetts; William Walker, Chicago; Yv Wathen, Davis, California; John Weber, Chicago; Clarence Wood, Philadelphia.

Many of these artists are active in mural centers, including: Artes Guadalupanos de Aztlan (Santa Fe), City Arts Workshop (New York), Freedom and Peace Mural Project (New York), Chicago Mural Group (Chicago), Casa Aztlan (Chicago), Puerto Rican Artists Association (Chicago), People's Painters (Highland Park, New Jersey), Mujeres Muralistas (San Francisco), Mechicano Art Center (East Los Angeles), City Wide Mural Painters (Los Angeles), Environmental Art, Philadelphia Museum of Art, and Galeria de la Raza (San Francisco).

Teachers and artists (many of whom have also directed murals) and experts in various fields who have further aided in the making of this manual are:

Mirron Alexandroff, Columbia College; Tom Allison, lawyer; Barbara Bernstein, writer; Janice Booker, professional typist; Paula Bower, elementary schoolteacher; John Bright, photographer; Deeks Carroll, high school art teacher; Esther Charbit, high school art teacher; Nancy Cohen, professional typist; Anna Marie Coveny, high school and college art teacher; Morton Curley, engineer; Don Eagleton, paint chemist who developed the paints section; Barry Gaither, National Center of Afro-American Artists, Boston; Susan Garber, Institute of Contemporary Art, Boston; Shirley Genther, Urban Gateways (Chicago); Elliot Hagel, insurance broker; Idelle Hammond, artist; Harold Haydon, artist and art critic; Kathleen Heim, reference librarian; Peter Hunt, Urban Dynamics (Chicago); Larry Hurlburt, art historian, who developed the bibliography; David Nebenzahl, graphic artist; Francis V. O'Connor, art historian; Elmer Olenick, musician and librarian; Mary Ott, elementary school art teacher; Bert Phillips, artist and art instructor; Helen Ratzer, Museum of Contemporary Art, Chicago; Anne Rogovin, special education teacher; Ellen Rogovin, elementary schoolteacher; Bob Solari, high school art teacher; Georg Stahl, architect; Leo Tanenbaum, design consultant; Ted Tanner, architect; Reni Templeton, artist; Linda Turner, professional typist; Ron Wheeler, Politic, Inc.; and Lester Wickstrom, cabinetmaker.

Tom Dorsey, photographer, deserves special thanks for his major photographic contributions to the manual. The illustrations have been prepared by Holly Highfill and Mark Rogovin.

The Authors

1 The Artist/Organizer

Most of the readers of this manual will find themselves in the role of artist/organizer for their mural project. Therefore, it's important for you, the reader, to consider the nature of this exciting, demanding, and important role. The artist/organizer is the person who keeps the whole project together. He or she seeks out community support and makes arrangements for supplies, finances, and documentation. He or she knows how to put together the content and the design and is responsible for directing the painting. The artist/organizer is sensitive to the people in the neighborhood and gives support and guidance to the team. In a school situation, the teacher who is organizing a mural project can be a gadfly. He or she can encourage other teachers to get mural projects growing out of social studies and other classes and can urge the school administration to expand and strengthen the art program in the school.

In some cases, the artist/organizer's role is to facilitate and encourage the work of student muralists. In other cases, the artist/organizer guides the development of the theme and the mural design -- making sure that the mural relates well not only to the team, but also to the general audience for the wall. The artist/ organizer does not always originate the mural project. A community center, for example, may want a mural in a particular location in the neighborhood and invite an artist to lead the project. An artist/organizer can be from either inside or outside the immediate community. In all cases, however, the artist/organizer assumes responsibility for setting and directing the work pattern for the project.

Painting before the public is a serious responsibility. A work of art put up in a public place will have an effect on the lives of the people who see it. For this reason, the artist/organizer must not go into a community with a "know-it-all" attitude. The artist/ organizer who is a true "public artist" takes more than a surface glance at the community to find themes to paint. He or she does research -- talks to community leaders, students, teachers, people on the street. The artist/organizer should try to find a constructive way to portray an issue -- How can the problem be solved? What are the ingredients for change? Don't look to downgrade or "slam" a community. At the same time, don't shy away from a controversial issue like racism. A mural can serve to educate and inspire a community. Confronting a community on an "unpopular" issue can and should be done in constructive ways. Public art effects change not by turning off viewers, but by challenging and involving them.

Becoming a public artist is not a matter of artistic talent alone, or of holding a degree. The public artist holds a position of responsibility, demanding serious thought and hard work on all aspects of the project, nonartistic as well as artistic.

1

SPONSORSHIP

An artist who sets out to start a mural project, whether from inside or outside the community, may wish to contact a neighborhood organization, a local political organization, a local church, school, or clinic, to sponsor the project. Local sponsorship is useful for several reasons. It can mean a closer link with the community, an avenue for getting supplies, help in building a team, possible salaries and stipends, and more. Sponsorship may also mean a certain amount of "control" over content by the sponsor -- so the artist should choose a sponsor carefully and keep in mind that the major objective is to relate a significant statement and work of art to the audience.

The next several chapters of this manual will deal primarily with procedures for painting outdoor community murals, in projects organized on a collective basis. Later the manual discusses classroom murals, portable murals, and other kinds of murals. But many of the ideas contained in the following chapters on collective outdoor murals can be applied to mural projects of all types, indoor or outdoor, permanent or portable, community-sponsored, or privately commissioned.

The order of events that we've outlined is not the only order to be followed. Each project is unique. The procedure will naturally vary with the special circumstances of your project.

1. Underpass mural

2 How to Select a Wall

A basic step in starting a mural project is to select the wall to paint on. In some cases, you may be doing a mural for a specific location -- in- or outside a clinic, a community center, or other institution. But if you do have a choice in selecting an outdoor wall, there are two main things to keep in mind. One is the *visibility of the location* -- the mural should, if possible, be on a wall that can be seen by a large number of people, especially since some murals take hundreds of hours to paint and involve many people. The *condition of the wall* is also very important, because this will greatly affect the life of the mural. Here are some more useful guidelines:

LOCATION

* walls on street corners are especially easy to see.

* walls that are at right angles to the street (facing traffic) are much more visible than walls facing the street. BUT make sure the view isn't blocked by another close building.

* don't choose a wall that faces away from traffic direction on a one-way street.

* don't choose a wall that's so low that it will be hidden by buses and parked cars.

* don't choose a wall space too high for the mural to be noticed.

* easily seen walls near bus and train intersections are good because they will be seen daily by large numbers of people. Other good locations are walls by playgrounds, entrance ways to schools, walls facing supermarket parking lots, gas stations, train tracks, and bus stops, and walls of community centers.

2.

3. Mural in stairwell

4. Mural in church

5. Mural in bank lobby

(AND DON'T FORGET the possibility of an indoor mural. Clinics, bus stations, libraries, churches, and many other places where people gather -- and often wait -- can be excellent locations for murals.)

6.

7. Mural in chapel

8. Freeway support

9. Recreation center

10. Bus bench

11. Park bandshell

12. Freestanding tower

SPECIAL TIP: If you have good alternatives, try to AVOID SOUTH-FACING WALLS. Prolonged exposure to the sun on a south wall can cause color fading and a faster breakdown of the paint film.

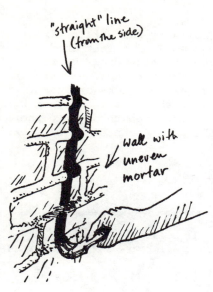

"straight" line (from the side)

wall with uneven mortar

CONDITION

- avoid walls with decaying, crumbling brick.

- watch out for brick walls with mortar that's loose, receding, or sticking out. Brick walls with mortar problems can soak up a lot of paint, and on a really bumpy wall straight lines are very difficult to paint.

- if you plan to paint on a brick wall, try to find one that's either new or repaired. If you have an old brick wall, try to get the landlord to *tuckpoint* it (repair and replace old mortar affected by years of weathering and other damage).

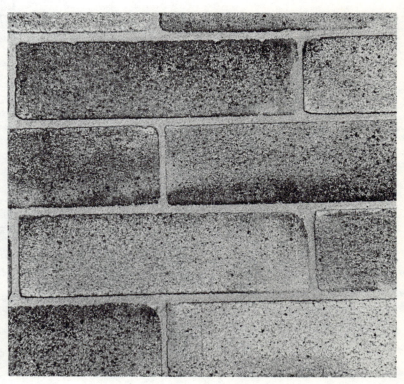

13.   14.

- watch out for moisture and drainage problems on brick walls.

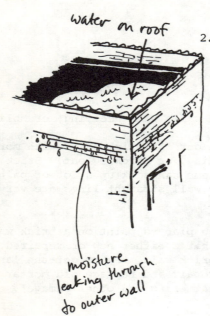

water on roof

moisture leaking through to outer wall

1. on walls where the brick goes right into the earth, with no barrier of cement or tar at the bottom, moisture is probably seeping from the ground up into the brick. This can damage the brick, causing it to crumble and harm your mural.

2. if the building has a false front or side (the wall goes up 3 or 4 feet above the roof), check the drainage from the roof. Also, make sure that the tar backing where the walls meet the roof has no cracks or leaks. If water is standing on the roof in contact with the brick, it can seep through to the outside and cause the paint to peel or blister.

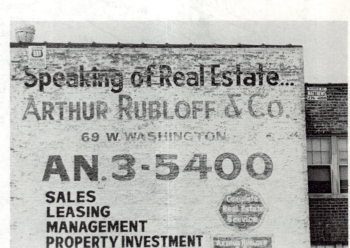

15. Extreme peeling on false roof section

- if you want to paint on a wall that's backed by earth -- as on an underpass under a railroad -- watch for water seepage or continual dampness. If such a problem is there, it will be a permanent problem with that wall. Be aware that it will eventually damage at least some areas of your mural.

- walls that are already painted (one color or with signs) should be in good condition -- not peeling or blistering. *You will inherit any paint problem that an already-painted wall may have.*

Make certain you can handle the wall you select. A smaller wall will diminish paint costs, time, scale problems, etc., and with a low wall you can reduce problems of scaffolding and insurance. *Don't get your hopes up over just one wall.* Line up several possibilities in case you don't get permission to use your first choice.

WARNING: Especially in urban renewal areas, check to see if the building you've selected is due to be torn down soon. If it is, you can decide whether or not to look for another wall. If you are not concerned about the mural's lasting for a long time and feel urgent about getting your message up immediately, you may choose to go ahead with the project. But if you know that your mural may soon be destroyed, you can plan to have a simple design that will not be a lot of work to complete.

16. Moisture leaking through underpass wall

17. Moisture affecting underpass mural

3   How to Get Permission

You must get permission from the owner of the building before you paint on a wall. Some owners are easy to locate, but some can be located only through the rental agent or realtor.

LOCATING THE OWNER

- the name of the landlord or the real estate company is often posted on or near the building.

- ask building tenants whom they pay their rent to.

- ask a community organization to find out who owns the building.

- look at the real estate tax rolls, under the street address, to find out who the owner is.

- in some cases, the building may be leased under a long-term lease. If so, it will probably be necessary to deal with the long-term lessee as well as with the owner.

You may have to locate two owners if you will be putting up ladders or scaffolding on someone else's property to reach your wall. *In some locations you may have to get permission from the city or township to put up scaffolding on public property like play-lots, park grounds, or sidewalks.*

APPROACHING THE OWNER OR AGENT

If you approach the landlord in person, it's important to sell the idea of the mural. *The owner is often concerned mainly with how the mural will affect the building's image in the community and its resale value.*

- point out that a mural is a good advertisement because it shows the landlord's concern for the community.

- suggest that in the case of some murals the property value has actually increased (it's true!).

- mention previous successful mural projects and show before-and-after photos of other murals. (Murals created by others can be used, in addition to examples of your own work, to make this point.)

- mention community supporters and sponsors of your project.

- take along a mutual friend, a tenant in the building, a respected community member, or someone else who will help achieve rapport with the owner.

- dress neatly, your aim is to paint a mural, not to pick a fight with a landlord.

WARNING: Sometimes the owner of a building will try to decide the theme. If it's a theme that you can work with, fine. But if you feel it's too restricting or a theme you're not interested in, try to convince the owner that the theme you've selected is worthwhile. If you can't reach a good agreement, it's better to look for other walls.

LEASING THE WALL

Permission that you get from the landlord usually *implies* a "gentlemen's agreement" that the owner will allow the mural to remain for a number of years. This informal agreement will at least make the landlord think twice before painting out or covering up the mural.

But a gentlemen's agreement is not legally binding, and it will have no effect on a future landlord if the building is sold. *If you have a building owner who is enthusiastic about the project,* see if he or she will *cooperate in drawing up a lease for the wall.* This lease, if worded properly (consult a lawyer), can be legally binding not only on the current owner, but also on "all future lessees, heirs, or purchasers" of the building. This means that even if the building is sold, no owner or tenant can destroy the mural for as long a period as has been specified in the lease. This kind of arrangement is often used for outdoor advertising.

Here are some suggested points to include in the lease:

- state who will be the holder of the lease (for instance, the artist/organizer or the sponsor of the mural project).

- name the present owner or long-term lessee of the building.

- state the exact location of the building, and which wall the lease applies to.

- state the date when the lease becomes effective.

- state the length of time that the lease will be in effect.

- state the amount of the rental fee -- suggest, for example, $1.00 a year. (There must be a money transaction for the lease to be legal, but this should be just a formality.) The fee can be paid in advance, for instance, at the dedication celebration.

- specify a money value for the mural, including the expenses for painting the mural. This specific money value will be an added deterrent to breaking the lease.

WALLS ON PUBLIC PROPERTY

If your wall is in a park, alongside a train track, or in an underpass, you will probably have to get permission from the city to paint on it. You or your sponsor should contact the local precinct captain or alderman to help you get permission.

- it may be necessary to obtain a permit from the city to "alter the outer appearance" of a building. It is probably better to consult a lawyer on this, instead of the city directly, to avoid being stopped short by red tape.

Don't be discouraged or give up if you are turned down. In fact, it's best if you don't pin all your hopes on one wall but have two or three other possible walls lined up. If you can't find any suitable wall in the area you want to do a mural in, you can consider doing a portable mural (see Chapter 11, "How to Do a Portable Mural"). But if a wall is especially good, bring more people (and new arguments) or more examples of your work and try to get the landlord to reconsider. Sometimes landlords just don't want to deal with new ideas and need a little push to seriously consider the prospect of a mural on their building.

18.

4 The Neighborhood Team

19.

One of the most important aspects of the neighborhood mural project is the organization of a neighborhood team to help plan and paint the mural. Especially if you are from outside the community, team members can be your most direct link with the immediate neighborhood. Your involvement with a team can solidify your commitment to the community. And the skills that everyone will learn on the project -- painting and designing skills and a chance to work together on a common project -- will substantially increase the value of the mural project in the community. *The way you organize the project can do much to create interest in the mural and encourage a serious response to the new work.*

Teams can be developed for a neighborhood project in a number of ways, depending on how the artist works, the artist/organizer's relation to and knowledge of the community, the size of the wall, the sponsor of the mural project, and the funds available.

Here are a few possible ways to begin recruiting a team:

● if you have a *community sponsor*, a local church or community center, they can recommend young people to work on the project.

- if you don't already have a sponsor, *talk to the director or art teacher of a community center* near the proposed wall. They can recommend young people for the project and may have their organization sponsor the project.

- *distribute a leaflet* throughout the community. Mention the mural site and the time, date, and place of planning meetings, and invite people to join in.

- contact the *art teacher or another interested teacher in a local school* about the project. Have the teacher recommend students to work with you after school, on weekends, or on vacation.
  Or you may be able to arrange with the teacher to have some of the students work on the mural for credit during school time.

Once you have a basic group together, you can count on the team's growing while the mural is being painted.

THE CORE GROUP

When you've begun to get a team together, watch for 3 or 4 team members who show special interest in and commitment to the project. These people can form the extremely important *core group* to share responsibility with you. The core group can:

- stay with you from the first discussions of the theme, through the painting, to the mural dedication.

- be a major source of ideas about the mural theme and how to paint it, especially if you are sensitive and listen carefully to their suggestions.

- help you by interviewing people on the street, circulating ideas, and asking for suggestions and criticisms throughout the neighborhood.

- help to build the rest of the team.

- watch out for safety on the project.

- be in charge of paints, brushes, equipment, and cleanup.

- in general, be responsible, with you, for the whole project, especially in terms of *serious artistic effort*, *showing up regularly*, etc.

It's very important to try to develop leadership qualities among the team members. Some of the core group will continue to work on other projects with you, or develop their own projects.

PLANNING MEETINGS

Begin work with the team by holding planning meetings. The main purpose of the planning meetings is for you and the team to discuss or develop the theme and develop a sketch. See Chapters 5 and 6, "How to Develop a Theme" and "How To Develop a Sketch," for detailed guidelines in these areas.

The planning meetings can also serve several additional purposes. They give you the opportunity to:

- *watch for people who might make up the core group.*

- find out the interests, art backgrounds, and talents of all the team members.

- *establish a base of operations.*

  1. hold planning meetings close to the proposed wall, in a room of a local church or community center.

  2. try to get the church or community center to let you continue to use their room to store paints, wash brushes, and hold meetings throughout the project.

  3. after the mural is completed, you may be able to persuade the center to set up an art program for team members and others who want to continue with art.

- *set a work schedule.* Set definite dates and times for painting, and work out areas of responsibility for each team member.

- *develop a feeling of collectivity.* Be sure to involve everyone in discussions of both the issues (content) of the mural and its design.

    Once the painting has begun, end-of-day evaluations, group lunches, and evening social gatherings can bring about a good spirit. Invite another muralist, a poet, or a community leader to join the team for a rap session over lunch.

If a good feeling is developed among the new team, team members will bring in friends and relatives. Once the drawing is up on the wall, others will come to help out. Some team members may be shy about expressing themselves artistically or politically at first, but will join in once some decisions are made.

5 How to Develop a Theme

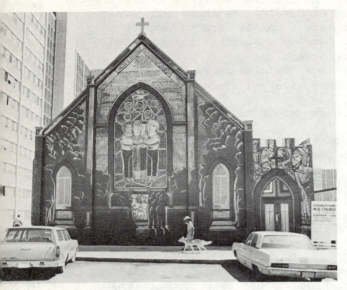

20. "All of Mankind," Chicago

The vital requirement for a mural theme is that it should have a definite relation to the community, to the people who will see it every day. A community can be a neighborhood, or any group of people with similar interests -- a school, a women's group, youth center, factory safety committee, housing project, consumer group.

Much thought, research, and care should be devoted to choosing a theme. After completion, the mural will be up in front of the community 24 hours a day, possibly for years. Make it worthwhile.

The theme can be political or social, dealing with issues of concern to the community like housing, child care, health care, rising prices, education, etc. It can be cultural, showing the history, the arts, and/or the daily life of the community. The theme can also be personal, a statement of deep feelings that the artist has a strong desire to express to the community -- feelings that the community can respond to.

Above all, the theme must speak to the community. If it doesn't, it has no place in the public forum of a mural.

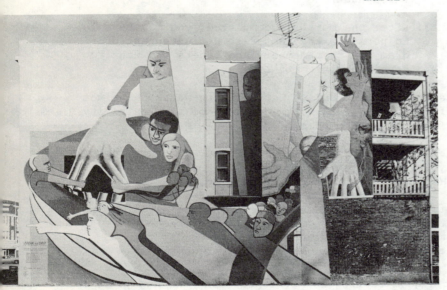

21. "Break the Grip of the Absentee Landlord," Chicago

23. "Sunburst," Chicago

22. "The Third Nail," Roxbury, Mass.

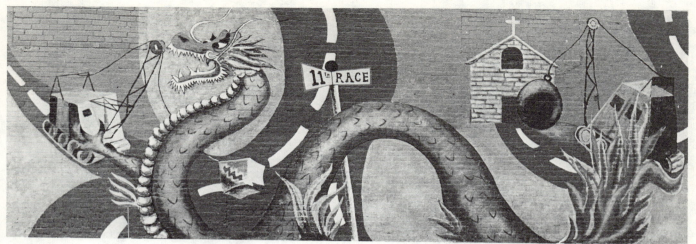

24. "Save the Chinatown Church," Philadelphia

25. "Liberty and Education," Santa Fe, N.M.

26. Detail, "Our Government Has Destroyed,
Our People Must Rebuild," East Berlin

19

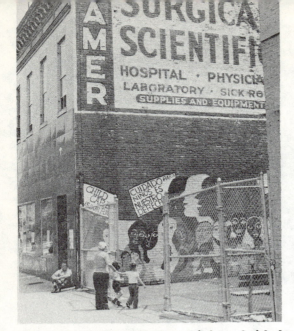

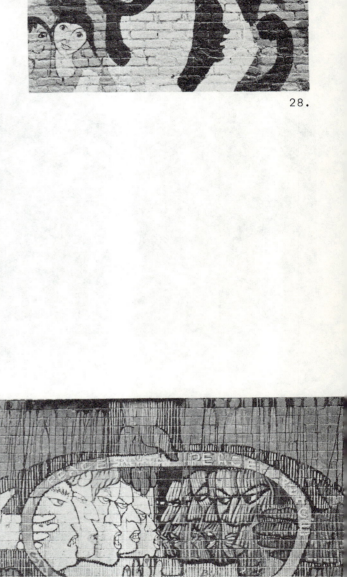

27. "Child Care Is Our Right--Cuidado Para Niños es Nuestro Derecho," New York

28.

29. "Wall of Respect," Chicago

30.

31.

Get to Know Your Audience

- talk to people in the community -- people on the street, community leaders, church groups, community organizations.

- read community literature -- neighborhood papers, community organization bulletins, etc.

- attend community meetings.

- find out from the community what issues are important.

- find out how (or whether) a theme you have in mind relates to feelings within the community.

REMEMBER: the mural is up before the public and not done just for you to see.

32. Detail, "History of Struggle in Pennsylvania," Philadelphia

Try to Make the Mural Theme a Group Decision

- if an organization is sponsoring your mural, see what ideas they have about a theme.

- involve your team in developing the theme.

- community leaders and activists can help develop a theme.

- *spend time drawing out the best ideas from the group.* Don't stop with the first idea suggested; develop that idea further and ask for other ideas.

- keep away from vague generalizations or trite statements -- pin down the issue.

- find out the local importance of a suggested theme -- how it affects the residents of the community where the mural is to be located, the core group, parents, schools, etc.

- keep in mind that the idea, whatever it is, has to be visualized. Try to end up with a statement that's clear and easily understood.

Special Pointers for Developing a Theme

- keep the public (your audience) in mind.

- simplify your theme. Don't drag in everything under the sun.

- the theme should be exciting and current. If it's a historical subject, try to link it up with something current.

- the location and setting of your mural (street corner, clinic, library) may help you determine the theme. Be sensitive to different types of places, and keep in mind that some themes will be inappropriate (ineffective, too) in some places.

For example, if your mural is in a child-care center, it should have a theme that would interest children and their parents. If your mural is in a clinic waiting room, it will need a different treatment than if it were on a busy street corner.

- in political and social murals, the artist and team can try to pose, within the mural, solutions to problems. This can make an especially positive, constructive work of art.

Even when your theme is decided on, stay open to the public. As people see the work in progress, they will contribute, help, suggest, advise. On a hot day, they'll bring refreshments. Everyone loves to watch the progress of a mural.

33. "The Crucifixion of Don Pedro Albizu Campos," Chicago

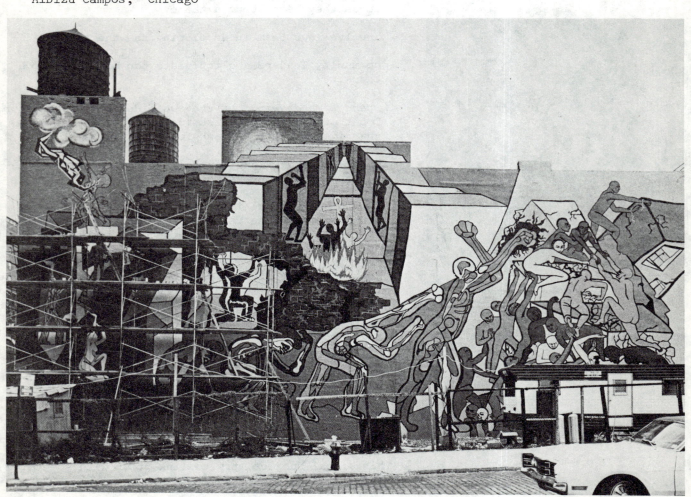

34. "Arise from Oppression," New York

There are two very important things to remember when you develop a sketch. One is the *location of the wall.* You have to know where your audience will be looking from and what the wall itself looks like. The other is *who your audience is.* You want to put across your theme in a way that your audience will understand and can relate to.

(See the end of this chapter for a suggested schedule to use when developing a sketch with a group.)

DEVELOP YOUR SKETCH WITH A SPECIFIC WALL IN MIND

- make your sketch the same general shape as that of the wall.

- take into account all the windows, doors, decoration, and other features already on your wall, and how they will affect the final appearance of the mural.

    (One way to make sure you are doing this is to measure and make a scale drawing of the blank wall and all its physical features -- placing windows, doors, etc., exactly. Make copies of this scale replica and develop your mural designs within it.)

- make the architectural features of your wall a positive part of the mural design. If you don't involve these features in your design, they will tend to be distracting. When viewers see a mural, they should not have to say, "Oh, there is a beautiful painting and also four windows." But beyond this, you can make the architectural features actually work to the mural's advantage. A creative involvement of windows, light wells, arches, etc., in the mural's design can weld the painting and the building together into a powerful three-dimensional work of art.

35. Incorporation of light well and window

- it's useful to have handy a photo of the wall when you're doing your sketch.

- note the "blind spots" on your wall -- places that are likely to be blocked out from the view of the public by traffic, parked cars, fences, buildings, or other obstacles.

  In your sketch, avoid these blind spots. Develop your main ideas in the most visible areas.

- take into account the immediate surroundings of the mural -- the rest of the building, other buildings, store signs, billboards, trees, etc. Try making a scale model of the wall and its immediate surroundings. As you work on your sketch, attach scale drawings of your ideas to the model wall. This will help you visualize how the mural will look in its surroundings.

- consider using an artistic style that will set the mural in contrast visually with its general surroundings. For example, a simple or plain style might work especially well in a cluttered, busy location.

- *find out from what angle and distance most viewers will see your mural. Make your sketch with this in mind.*

  1. figures and other images should be large enough to be seen easily from a distance.

  2. if your wall is very high (3 or more stories), adjust the perspective in your sketch so that the mural will make sense to the people on street level.

- figure out how much time viewers will have to see the mural. Will they be riding past it in a car or on the train, or is it in a place where viewers can walk past or sit down and take a long time to look?

  1. *immediate impact mural.* If the viewer has only a few seconds to see the mural (for example, if most viewers will see it from a bus, train, or car), make your design simple, bold, and easily understood, for *immediate impact.*

36. Immediate impact mural, "Protect the Peoples' Homes," Chicago

24

2. *contemplative mural*. If the viewer has plenty
of time to see the mural (perhaps in a clinic or
a bus station), you can design a *contemplative*
mural (one you stand and look at and think
about). This can be visually and symbolically
more complex. It can demand much more from the
viewer.

● if your wall is in a *hard-to-notice place* (for example small and high up), the mural might have simple
or bold movements and contrasting color tones to
catch the viewer's attention.

37. Contemplative mural, "Peace and
Salvation, Wall of Understanding,"
Chicago

KNOW YOUR AUDIENCE — PUBLIC AND PRIVATE SYMBOLISM

Know the culture and expectations of the audience that will see your mural when you develop the sketch.

● don't use images or a style that are offensive or meaningless to your audience. This naturally will vary from community to community.

● use symbols that can be understood by the specific audience. Above all, avoid *private symbolism*.
   Private symbolism speaks to a clique, an "in group," or an elite. It can also be strictly personal to the artist. The art works that contain private symbolism cannot be understood by the majority of people who see them. In too many cases, the artist has no interest in speaking to anyone but friends. Some even have contempt for the general public, feeling that their ideas are too lofty to be understood by everyone.
   Public symbolism speaks to a general audience. The symbols require no special art training to be understood. Thus an art work using public symbolism can be understood by the vast majority of its audience -- whether the audience is a specific ethnic grouping or community, or the general public.
   (Within the general category of public symbolism are those specific symbols, like the peace sign, the raised fist, religious symbols, etc., that have a generally understood meaning on their own. These very specific symbols are almost like words -- they can be used in combination to form a "symbolic sentence" or unified meaning. If you use these kinds of symbols in a mural, make sure they work artistically and thematically with the rest of the work, and are not just "stuck in.")

● *talk to people*. Test yourself while you're developing sketch, and later while you're working on the wall. Ask passers-by to explain the meaning of your mural. Make sure their interpretation is what you had in mind.

● even personal themes can be painted in such a way that your ideas will be open for all to understand.

39. Detail, peace symbol from "Wall of Brotherhood," Chicago

SPECIAL TIPS FOR DEVELOPING THE SKETCH

● be sure that the sketch is in a style that all the team members can paint. A style that involves a lot of sophisticated modeling, shading, or complex detail may be difficult for your team to paint. Also, a style that involves a highly personalized brush stroke will be hard to imitate. Be aware of what is possible for your team.
   If your team members have some painting skills, they can handle a more complex and more personal style.

40. Detail, "I.O.U.," Chicago

41. Detail, "Let a People Loving Freedom, Come to Growth," New York

42. Detail, "400 Years of Struggle," New York

27

43. Detail, "Jamestown Mural,"
San Francisco

44. Detail, "Hay Cultura en Nuestra
Comunidad," Chicago

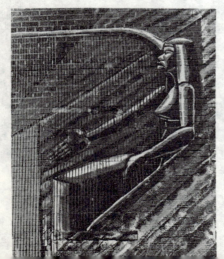

45. Detail, "Wall of Meditation,"
Chicago

46. Artist at work, "Rip Off," Chicago

47. Detail, "Black Man's Dilemma," Chicago

48. Detail, "Nation Time," Chicago

49. Sketch for "Wall of Brotherhood," Chicago

50. "Wall of Brotherhood," Chicago

51. Graffiti on "The Plumed Serpent," Los Angeles

● try to *make your sketch as final and complete as possible*. It's easier to erase a mistake on the sketch than on the wall. *Large changes on the wall will take up much time and paint.*

● you might *seek advice from experienced mural painters* before considering your sketch final -- especially if it's your first mural. What seems fine in a small sketch might not work out well on a large scale. It often takes much experience to know how to design for a large wall. Even experienced mural painters benefit from the fresh viewpoint of other muralists.

● use color markers (Magic Markers, oil crayons, pastels, colored chalk, etc.) to define large color areas.

● color wheels and color cards from a paint store can help you and the team select colors and see how colors will look next to each other.

● think of color as a way to get across a certain feeling or idea.

    1. sometimes *colors act as symbols* that have definite political or religious meanings.

    2. color may also be used as an expression of emotion. For example, many people think of blood a and fire when they see red -- so a strong red in a mural could give a general feeling of violence or passion. Green could be used to suggest life and growth.

● *be careful about using words*. Some murals have skillfully involved poetry and other writing with a good effect. But in other cases, words have been used as a crutch, to avoid having to make the statement visually. And very often words in a mural are not part of the total visual design.

    If the idea you want to get across can be said without using words, it can be more effective. Often familiar or overused slogans are not contemplated by the viewer, but just read off without thinking.

● if there is a lot of *graffiti* being done in your area and you think your mural might become defaced with graffiti, *try to deal with the situation creatively*.

    1. if your mural project shows real concern for the neighborhood, and the mural is a real expression of feelings in the neighborhood (including the feelings of youth in the area), the problem of graffiti may very well never come up.

    2. people who have worked on a project are not likely to deface it, so if there is a particular group (like a neighborhood gang) that might do graffiti on the mural, try to recruit them into the project.

3. if you think that there is no way to avoid having graffiti on your mural, try designing the mural to incorporate it -- create areas (probably near the bottom of the mural) in which graffiti can go without destroying the design. The graffiti may even contribute to your theme and design.

4. some mural groups have used a "graffiti guard" -- a clear, high-gloss coating of "solution acrylic" (see the paint chart in Chapter 8, "Paints and Wall Preparation") over the mural. This will make spray-paint graffiti fairly easy to clean off.

• if there is *more than one place from which a large number of people will see the mural*, try to aim your design toward all these viewing points, not just one.

• *political murals should be artistically strong.* This will go a long way toward involving the viewer in thinking about the mural's message. Even people who are indifferent to the mural's statement may be won over if it's a beautiful work.

• *most decisions that you will make about colors, placement of forms, etc., will be determined by both aesthetic and content considerations.* Don't destroy a good design by sticking in an issue where it doesn't fit visually. On the other hand, don't weaken the statement of issues by forcing it into an artistic design that will overshadow, obscure, or distort the content. Make your decisions a blend of both aesthetics and content, so that the mural can be excellent in both areas, and both areas can work together.

GROUP PROCEDURE FOR DEVELOPING A SKETCH

Group development of the sketch by the team brings a wide range of ideas and a greater involvement of the team with the mural. Even if the artist/organizer ends up doing most of the work on the final sketch, ideas and involvement of the team will be valuable for everyone concerned. But the sketch does not necessarily have to be a group effort. If circumstances call for it, the artist/organizer can develop the sketch alone. In any case, be sure you make clear from the beginning whether the decision on the sketch is to be yours alone or a collective one. Don't ask your team for suggestions and then disappoint them by ignoring them.

Usually at least 3 sessions are needed for a group project before the theme is worked out and the final sketch is produced (some groups use as many as 8 sessions or more). Here's a suggested schedule for one way of planning the project with your team (meetings could be held on 3 Saturdays in a row).

First Session

- look at pictures or slides of murals, or take a car tour of murals in the area, to give the team a better idea of what a mural is.

- use a local library or downtown public library to look at pictures of wall paintings from the past -- 20th century Mexican murals, New Deal murals of the 1930s, Michelangelo's Sistine Chapel, Giotto's frescoes, Byzantine mosaics, etc. Although some of the team members may be familiar with today's murals, few will have much knowledge of art from the past. A look at earlier wall painting will be inspiring because it shows that the team is working in an old and great tradition.

- develop/discuss the theme (see Chapter 5, "How to Develop a Theme," and Chapter 1, "The Artist/Organizer").

- ask everyone to bring drawings that illustrate the agreed-upon theme to the next meeting.

- have everyone make their drawings the same shape as that of the wall -- or draw the outline of the wall on *large* sheets of paper and pass them out for people to sketch on.

- if people can't draw, or are afraid to draw, they can bring in magazine pictures or newspaper clippings to illustrate their ideas. Or the team might act out ideas and photograph the results.
  Also, verbal descriptions of possible mural designs can be quite valuable.

- set the time and place for the next meeting.

Second Session

- review discussion of the theme.

- look over drawings.

- select drawings that have ideas that can be combined in a final sketch.

- try to select one drawing that has a basic design (composition) into which the other ideas can be combined.

Third Session

- develop the final sketch. Remember, it is important always to consider the feelings, involvement, and talent of the team in handling decisions about the sketch. Developing the final sketch can be handled in several ways; for example:

1. the artist/organizer and the person who came up with the basic drawing could finalize the sketch together.

2. the artist/organizer could take all the drawings and ideas and use them to finalize the sketch on his or her own.

3. one of the team members could finalize the sketch.

- decide on colors.

- set a schedule for working on the wall.

OTHER KINDS OF MURALS

There are no set rules as to how to develop a mural project. Below are different kinds of projects and different ways of developing projects -- other than the collective mural under the direction of an artist/organizer.

- ARTIST AND ASSISTANTS. One artist can develop a sketch and direct a project with the other artists as assistants.

- COLLABORATION AMONG ARTISTS. A small group of artists can work together in developing and executing a mural. This can be difficult, especially if the styles of the artists differ widely. But it can also be very rewarding if there is a workable combination of styles and skills within the group.

- SECTION PER ARTIST. The wall can be divided into sections among a group of artists. Each can paint a section -- sometimes with a common overall theme.

- GRAPHICS MURAL. A simple picture (like a poster design, a political emblem, or a news photograph) can be blown up with an opaque projector or other means and traced on a wall. Graphics murals can be produced very quickly.

- SUNDAY AFTERNOON MURAL.

1. get permission to paint a low wall or fence.

2. leaflet the community and invite anyone to join in painting a common theme.

3. **bring** paints, brushes, mixing cans, and drop-cloths and be on hand to help with the project.

52. "Peoples' Handshake," Chicago

53. Construction fence, Hamilton, Ontario, Canada

- MURAL DESIGN CONTEST. A building owner or community center can sponsor a contest to submit designs for a certain wall. The contest winner, in consultation with other muralists, can then do the project, possibly involving a team.

- GUERRILLA MURAL. A highly organized, fast-working group of people can use "guerrilla" techniques to paint not only slogans, but sophisticated artistic/political statements -- on walls, fences -- almost anywhere. Pre-planning and the use of such techniques as spray guns or stencils are very desirable for the success of this kind of mural.

- PRIVATE COMMISSIONS. Unions, churches, community centers, libraries and other institutions, and private individuals sometimes commission individual artists or groups of artists to do a mural for their own buildings. With a private commission, your patron may give you a specific theme, or may leave it up to you.

- SILHOUETTE MURAL, PAPER MURAL, MOSAIC, CUT-PAPER MURAL. See Chapter 10, "The Classroom Mural," Chapter 11, "How to Do a Portable Mural," and Chapter 12, "How to Do a Mural on Cloth."

54. Detail, "Rio Mapocho Mural," Santiago Chile, painted before the coup in 1973

7 Transferring the Sketch to the Wall

Blowing up your sketch onto the wall or other mural surface should not be seen only as a mechanical process. Be willing to change the drawing if what you have drawn doesn't work well on the large surface. But to reproduce the basic lines of your sketch accurately on a large scale, here are several different methods that you may use:

Make a Grid

* measure the exact dimensions of your wall.

* make your drawing the same shape as the wall so that the grid will correspond exactly.

* make your drawing of some convenient size -- for example, so that one inch in the drawing equals one foot on the wall. (If the wall is, for instance, 24 feet high and 30 feet long, it simplifies things to make the drawing 24 inches high and 30 inches wide.)

* draw a grid on top of your sketch (or on a sheet of clear plastic to be placed over your sketch). A grid is a series of equally spaced vertical lines -- going from top to bottom, and horizontal lines -- going from left to right.
  The lines of the grid form small squares on the sketch that correspond with large square areas on the wall. For example, if you make your lines one inch apart, you will have a series of one-inch squares that can correspond to areas of one square foot on the wall.
  You don't *have* to make one inch in your sketch correspond to one foot on the wall. If you have a huge wall you may want to have one inch in your sketch correspond with 3 or 4 feet on your wall. *Or* if you have a very small wall, make two-inch squares on your sketch to correspond to one-foot squares on the wall. Your scale sketch should be large enough so that you can easily see and define details.

* number and letter your lines -- vertical lines A,B, C,D, etc., horizontal lines 1,2,3,4, etc. -- for easy reference.

* make the same grid on the wall. Use a snap line to make long straight lines on the wall (see Chapter 21, "Helpful Hints").
  If you have a good-sized wall, it's useful to use two or more colors of chalk for your lines. You can make every fifth line a different color, for example, to help you keep from losing your place on the wall. *Or* you can break areas of the wall into smaller grids for drawing in details, and put the small-scale grid lines in different colors from the main grid.

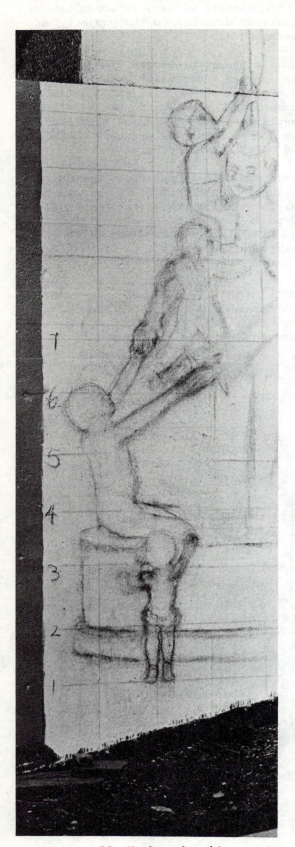

55. Numbered grid on wall

REMEMBER: the mural is the work of art, not the sketch or an idea in the mind, so the mural must speak for itself.

- draw in on the large squares on the wall what appears on the small squares in your sketch.

- stand back often as you draw on the wall to make sure the drawing looks right from a distance.

- BE FLEXIBLE. If your drawing on the wall follows the grid but doesn't look right from a distance, change it.

- watch out for irregular brickwork, holes in the wall, or ridges, etc. If an important detail in your design turns out to be on or right next to an obstacle of this kind, try to shift it over some. Otherwise the obstacle will distort or distract the eye away from the painted detail.

Many artists use a grid only to get the major lines and movements on the wall. Then they fill in the details and make adjustments by eye.

Use Natural Markers on the Wall

There are two methods for blowing up a sketch that make use of the natural features of the wall -- windows, doors, bricks, tiles, brick decoration.

The *first method* is a variation on the simple grid:

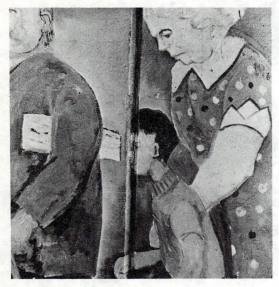

56. Shift the drawing slightly to avoid an obstacle

57. Sketch for "Unity of the People," Chicago

58. Blow up of the sketch onto the wall

59. Mural in progress

- *to make your horizontal lines:* Count the bricks going up the side of the wall. Divide the number of bricks in half, thirds, quarters, or whatever. Draw lines horizontally across the row of bricks at each of these points.

- *to make your vertical lines:* If there are evenly spaced objects at the top of the wall, such as decorative tiles, coping tiles, lights, etc., you can use these to space off your vertical lines. (Coping tiles are protective tiles at the top of many brick walls -- there is a knob on the end of each of the tiles, approximately 17 inches apart.)

Coping tiles (draw a line down from every other tile)

bricks

(divide the number of bricks by 3 and draw lines across to make 3 equal sections)

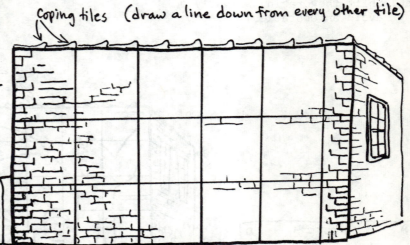

- these horizontal and vertical lines will form a grid on the wall.

- make a sketch the same shape as that of the wall.

- mark on your sketch where the wall features (bricks, tiles, etc.) should appear, according to scale.

- using these features as a guide, make lines on your sketch, like those on the wall, to form a grid.

36

- then transfer your sketch, as with an ordinary grid, back onto the wall.

The *second method* using natural features of the wall can be used with *more complicated walls* -- walls with a lot of windows, doors, decoration, drainpipes, etc.:

- measure the size and placement of the natural markers such as windows, doors, and decorative borders on your wall.

- make a scale drawing, or map, of these natural markers.

- trace this "map of the wall" on top of your sketch, or -- better yet -- develop your sketch around these natural markers in the first place (see Chapter 6, "How to Develop a Sketch").

- use the natural markers on the wall as reference points when you draw in your basic design on the wall.

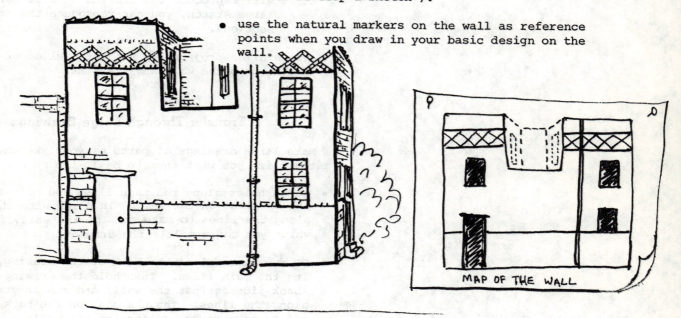

MAP OF THE WALL

Project Your Sketch onto the Wall

If you want to project your sketch, you will have to work either at night (for an outdoor mural) or in a darkened room (for an indoor mural).

- *use an opaque projector*. Go over the main forms in your sketch with a dark, heavy line. Then project this heavy line drawing, or parts of it, onto the wall. Trace the main forms in your design onto the wall and fill in the rest freehand. (You can also use the opaque projector to project drawings and photographs from newspapers, magazines, and books.)

  1. if your wall and design are large, the sketch can be projected in sections.

2. make sure that the projector is directly in front of the section of the wall on which you want the image to appear, to avoid keystoning (distortion) of the image.

- *use an overhead projector*. Draw your sketch on transparent plastic and project and trace it on the wall as with an opaque projector.

    1. take the same precautions against distortion, etc., as you would with an opaque projector.

    2. if you have the equipment available, you can make your transparencies not by drawing onto the plastic, but by making acetate transparencies. Make a photo copy of the drawing and then run this copy through a thermoacetate machine, which will reproduce the drawing in acetate. For a large sketch, you can reproduce the drawing in sections.

- *use a slide projector*. Project a slide of your sketch onto the wall and trace it.

Transfer Through Large Drawings

Make large drawings of parts of your sketch, the actual size you want them to be in the mural.

- punch holes along the main lines and hold the drawing in place on the wall. Then rub with chalk along the lines to make dots on the wall, from which you can complete the drawing.

- OR rub charcoal on the back of the drawing, following the main lines. Then hold the drawing in place (back side against the wall) and rub or draw hard along the lines. The charcoal on the back will come off to make marks or lines on the wall.

For both these methods, you need a relatively smooth wall.

8   Paints and Wall Preparation

This chapter is about the technical aspects of paints and wall preparation. It's divided into five sections: a chart showing how to prepare and paint different kinds of walls, a section on how to interpret a commercial paint label analysis, a discussion of artists' acrylic paints, a section on selecting and mixing paint colors, and a glossary of terms. Some of the information in this chapter is, we feel, essential to good mural painting. Some is very technical and will probably not concern everyone. But we have tried to include as much useful information as possible for people to use as they want and need it. And we realize that funds are often the determining factor. Even if it's impossible for you to follow even our strongest recommendations -- for types of paints, etc. -- this should *not* keep you from going ahead with whatever means are available to you. *But if you have a choice, it's extremely worthwhile to take a little extra trouble to prepare your wall properly and use the right paints and the best you can afford.* Especially, we would like to emphasize the often read and often disregarded instruction on every paint can label: "The surface must be free of dirt, grease, loose paint, etc." It takes little time or expense to follow this instruction, but it will make a tremendous difference in the eventual condition of your mural.

We have emphasized commercial housepaints over artists' paints in this chapter, the foremost reason being that commercial paints are less expensive than artists' paints. Another reason is that, for outdoor murals, technical information on the performance of artists' paints is incomplete. Although some artists report that some brands of artists' acrylics, for example, stand up very well outside, we know also that many artists' acrylic paints may not stand up well -- because they have not been formulated for outdoor use. (See the section on artists' acrylic paints.) On the other hand, we have observed that the better commercial exterior housepaints do last from 4 to 6 years or even longer because they are the result of years of research into durability, light resistance, etc. We urge everyone, however, to experiment and to continue to investigate other supplies that might be useful for mural painting -- see Chapter 13, "Other Techniques/Durability."

Some of the mural painters have used specific brands with success on outdoor walls. Most nationally advertised brands of commercial paint are satisfactory in terms of durability, etc. If you want to work in enamel paint, we have found that Sign Painter's One Shot Bulletin is very good. It covers in one coat and comes in an unusually good range of strong, bright colors. If you can afford it, we have also found that Politec brand artists' acrylics (produced in Mexico and California and used by many of the leading Mexican muralists) do very well outside; artists' acrylics in general have colors of superior purity and brilliance.

Brick, Concrete, Cement Block, Stucco, Adobe

WALL PREPARATION	PRIMER	PAINT	REMARKS
Exterior 1. Remove all loose material (dirt, grease, crumbled brick and mortar, and, if the wall has been previously painted, any loose paint) by scraping, brushing with a wire brush or broom, or sand blasting. 2. If there are large cracks in the wall (as often happens with old brick walls that have been overlaid with concrete), fill in the cracks with a pre-mixed sand and cement filler, such as "Sacrete" (available at most hardware stores). This is to keep water from getting into the cracks, freezing in winter and expanding and creating bigger holes. Before applying filler, roughen the brick with a pick or chisel and soak the area with water. 3. If present, treat efflorescence (a white, powdery chemical deposit that accumulates on bricks) by sponging affected areas of the wall with a solution of zinc sulfate (1 lb. to 2 gallons of water). Zinc sulfate is available at most chemical supply houses and some hardware stores. (Ask for "technical grade" zinc sulfate, which is 99 percent pure and much less expensive than the chemically pure substance.) 4. Check the coping tile at the top of the wall and the caulking around window and door sills. If they are loose, recaulk to keep water from getting in behind the paint primer.	If the surface is already painted and in good condition, you don't need to prime it. If not, use an exterior or interior latex housepaint primer, either acrylic or poly-vinyl acrylic *or* use a pliolite-based masonry primer or conditioner (a primer with a rubber binder specially made for masonry). WARNING: *Never use an oil or alkyd base primer on masonry. In the presence of moisture, alkaline elements in the wall will cause a breakdown of oil or alkyd base primer.*	Use an exterior latex housepaint, either acrylic or poly-vinyl acrylic. *or* use exterior oilbase housepaint or exterior enamel paint (*only over a primer -- see IN-TERIOR, below*) *or* use artists' acrylic paint.	If the wall is too rough, a latex block filler (a heavy, paste-like substance) can be used to fill in the holes. Apply with brush or roller and wet trowel to a smooth finish. If you want to create a textured surface, roughen the wet block filler with a broom, crumpled paper, or a sponge. If you cover the entire wall surface with block filler, you don't need a primer. If the wall has been previously painted with a gloss paint, dull the old paint surface with steel wool or sandpaper so that your paint coat will stick to it well. If the old paint is peeling, you may want to feather (smooth down) the edges of the old paint film with a wire brush. (Try using a wire brush attachment on an electric drill to cut down on the work.) This is usually worthwhile only on a rather smooth wall where the edge of the old paint is very visible. If there is earth (rather than concrete) at the base of the wall, you can minimize paint peeling at the bottom of the wall by digging a trench (1' by 1') along the base to keep rain water from soaking up into the wall. Slant the trench toward the street or an alley (so the water will run off) and fill the trench with gravel.

WALL PREPARATION	PRIMER	PAINT	REMARKS
If the wall rises above the level of the roof, make sure that the flashing (tar sealer between the roof and the wall) is intact to keep the water on the roof from leaking into the wall.			
Interior Same as for exterior.	If the wall is in good condition, either painted or unpainted, there is no need to prime it unless you are using oil base paint. If the wall is not in good condition, or if you are going to use an oil base paint, prime it with interior latex flat or semi-gloss primer. NOTE: Adobe walls, if unpainted, should be primed with a latex primer.	Use interior latex flat or semi-gloss paint *or* use artists' acrylic paint *or* use interior oil base housepaint or enamel paint. WARNING: *If you use any oil or alkyd base paint, including enamel, you must prime the wall first* to prevent a breakdown of the paint resulting from direct contact with moisture and alkaline elements in the wall.	*Primer and Paint* Commercial acrylic paints and primers are more durable (weather- and light-resistant) than polyvinyl acrylic paints and primers, but polyvinyl acrylics are cheaper than acrylics. Both are good to use, however. Artists' acrylics have truer, more uniform, and more intense color, and are more opaque (nontransparent) than commerical paints, but there is a danger of fading with some pigments. (See section on artists' acrylic paints in this chapter.) Good commercial housepaints are usually tougher and are formulated not to fade. Certain primers and paints don't mix. Make sure that the ones you use will go together (ask a paint dealer), and stay with one company's products whenever possible. *Sealer* If you have used the right kind of paint, a sealer is usually not necessary for durability. But a sealer of clear varnish can give a shine to a dull (matte) surface. On an indoor wall, use a thin coat of sealer to minimize yellowing. *Don't use ordinary varnish on an outdoor wall.* It will crack, peel, and possibly discolor.

WALL PREPARATION	PRIMER	PAINT	REMARKS
			If you feel it necessary to put a sealer over an outdoor mural, use a solution acrylic, a clear liquid plastic coating to which ingredients have been added that absorb ultraviolet light. Several manufacturers produce such a product. (One is called Uvitron Protective Sealer.) NOTE: Solution acrylic can be used easily over latex housepaints and oil-base enamel, but with some other oil-base paints (which have a long curing time) the solution acrylic may blister the paint surface if the paint is not thoroughly cured. If you are using a flat or semi-gloss oil-base housepaint, test the solution acrylic on a small portion of the mural to see if it has cured long enough to take it. *Apply sealer only with a brush -- a roller is likely to create air bubbles that will fog the sealer when it dries.*

WOOD

Plywood, Masonite, Particle Board

Exterior			*Primer and Paint*
Remove dirt, grease, etc., and, if the wall has been previously painted, any loose paint. If there is an old paint coat and the surface is glossy, dull it with steel wool or sandpaper so your paint coat will stick to it well.	If wall is painted and in good condition, there is no need to prime. If not, prime with exterior latex housepaint primer, either acrylic or polyvinyl acrylic or	Use exterior latex housepaint, either acrylic or polyvinyl acrylic or use artists' acrylic paints	For differences between the different types of primers and paints, see *REMARKS* under "Masonry." *Sealer* See *REMARKS* under "Masonry."

WALL PREPARATION	PRIMER	PAINT	REMARKS
	exterior oil or alkyd base primer. Be sure to *prime the edges of the wood,* if exposed, and the *insides of cracks,* preferably with **two** coats of primer.	or use exterior enamel or exterior oil base housepaint.	
Interior Same as for exterior.	If painted and in good condition, you don't need to prime. If not, use latex enamel primer or oil or alkyd base primer. WARNING: Don't use latex paint over oil or alkyd base primer. It will not stick well.	Use interior latex flat or semigloss paint unless you have used an oil or alkyd base primer or use artist's acrylic paints or use interior oil base housepaint or high gloss enamel or sash-and-trim enamel. Use enamel where there will be much traffic or wear.	

SPECIAL SURFACES

Glazed Brick, Glass, Ceramic Tile, Formica

Clean: For cleaning off simple dirt, use a common cleanser such as Fantastic, Soilax, Mr. Clean, Windex for glass, etc. For cleaning off heavy grease, etc., use a solution of trisodiumphosphate -- 3 tablespoons to 2 gallons of water. (Trisodiumphosphate is available at a hardware store.)	*Adhesion of the paint is the critical factor here.* Use of an ordinary primer will almost certainly result in peeling of the paint surface. Use only an acrylic organisol solution primer such as Elliot's Tite Bond or Pratt and Lambert Adheron.	Same as for exterior and interior masonry.	

HOW TO INTERPRET A COMMERCIAL PAINT LABEL ANALYSIS

Most reputable paint manufacturers include on the label of each can of paint a product analysis describing the contents of the can. (A rule of thumb is to regard cans of paint that do not have a label analysis as possibly inferior products.)

Being able to understand a label analysis can help you select a better product and may save you money. Almost all paints are made up of two major categories of ingredients:

1. "pigment": including the true pigment or coloring agent and various other substances added to achieve durability and easy brushing, etc., and

2. "vehicle": including the true vehicle -- an oil or synthetic film former that binds the pigment to the wall -- plus a tiny percentage of chemicals added to slow drying, etc., and a volatile (evaporating) solvent, usually, mineral spirits or water, that thins the paint and evaporates as the paint dries.

The key thing to look for in reading a label analysis is how much of your money is going to pay for paint that stays on the wall (pigment, durability and drying substances, and true vehicle) and how much is going to pay for the volatile solvent that evaporates and is of relatively little use to you. Often "bargain paints" are loaded with evaporating solvent, so that it might take twice as much "bargain paint" to cover the same area as it would a more expensive paint in another brand or a different line of the same brand.

REMEMBER: The precentages of ingredients in paints are different for different types of products, depending on whether they are gloss, semi-gloss, or flat paints, latex or oil-base paints, etc. So comparisons should be made only between two products of the same type.

Here is a typical product analysis for a latex paint as it might appear on the label of a can:

Pigment		51%
Titanium dioxide	50%	
Silicates	10	
Calcium carbonates	40	
	100%	
Vehicle		49%
Polyvinyl acetate	49%	
Glycols and surface active agents	3	
Water	48	
	100%	100%

There are two ways to figure out how much solvent (water) you have: by percentage and by weight.

1. You know that the large category of pigment substances makes up 51 percent of the product and the large category of vehicle substances

makes up 49 percent of the product. Of that 49 percent made up by the vehicle substances, the solvent (water) makes up 48 percent. So the solvent is 23.5 percent (.48 times 49) of the total product.

2. If the weight of the entire can of paint is, for example, 10 pounds, then the pigment part weighs 5.1 pounds (10 times .51), and the vehicle part weighs 4.9 pounds (10 times .49). The solvent (water) is 48 percent of 4.9 pounds, or 2.35 pounds (4.9 times .48).

When you know how much of the product is solvent, you can compare the solvent content in that product with the solvent content in the same product in other brands to find the best quality paint in your price range.

SELECTING AND MIXING PAINT COLORS

The muralist has a special problem in getting paints in a good range of useful colors. Conventional artists' paints are expensive to buy. On the other hand, it's hard to get a useful and complete range of colors in the less expensive commercial housepaints. Since most paint manufacturers don't market paints specifically for mural painting, it is necessary to improvise.

The easiest way to buy commercial paints is to select colors from a color chart published by the paint manufacturer and buy quantities of each color. But this can present problems. Often, especially with latex paints, you won't find all the colors you need on the color chart. This is because, except with enamels, paint manufacturers sell mainly pastel, off-color shades that are popular with homeowners for painting walls, rather than the truer, stronger colors that artists use. There is a special problem if you want to mix additional colors from the colors that you've purchased -- you need fairly true shades of color to achieve good results from mixing.

One way to get a wider and better range of colors is to have your colors specially mixed. Most large paint dealers can do this for you, using a new color system that has been developed by paint manufacturers. This involves using a series of bases, containing solvent (thinner) and vehicle (film-former that binds the pigment to the wall). To these are added combinations of small amounts of high-intensity colorants (concentrations of pigment) to make different color shades of paint. This color system can be used to mix almost any color imaginable, and bases and colorants come in most common types of paint -- interior and exterior latex, oil-base paints, enamels, wood stains, etc. The paint dealer can either mix all the colors you think you'll need, or mix enough basic colors (red, blue, yellow, green, and brown) for you to combine into different shades as you need them.

Mixing Your Own Paints

Finally, people who want to take the time and make the effort can mix their own colors using the colorants and bases system -- most colorants and bases can be purchased unmixed. If you know what you are doing, this is the best way to get exactly the colors that you want. We have listed some of the most common bases and colorants with a description of their properties as a guide for those who want to attempt mixing their own colors. (Consultation with a paint chemist from a paint company or an experienced painter is also recommended for beginners.)

Here is a list of some of the commonly used bases and colorants:

Bases

Light Tint Bases -- designed to produce pale shades in all colors. Very similar to regular white paint and very opaque (nontransparent). 1 gallon of this type of base takes up to 8 fluid ounces of colorant.

Deeptone Bases -- designed to produce colors in medium tones. These contain less white pigment than the light tint bases and thus allow deeper colors to be made. 1 gallon takes up to 8 fluid ounces of colorant.

Ultra-Deep Bases -- designed to produce very deep tones in all colors except deep reds and yellows. 12 fluid ounces of colorant per gallon of base.

Yellow Bases -- for producing moderately deep colors from red-orange through blue-green (red-orange, orange, yellow-orange, yellow, yellow-green, green, blue-green). 12 fluid ounces of colorant per gallon of base.

Red Bases -- for producing reddish colors from maroon through red-orange to brown. 12 fluid ounces of colorant per gallon of base.

Charcoal Bases -- for producing muted or muddy shades in all colors. 12 fluid ounces of colorant per gallon of base.

Colorants

Be sure to ask for *universal machine-type colorants.*

1. Hansa Yellow -- a clear, primary (medium) yellow with a green undertone.

2. Carbon Black -- a very opaque black with a blue undertone.

CAUTION: If you buy bases and colorants to mix your own paints, buy all materials in the SAME BRAND.

NOTE: The yellow bases and red bases produce a greater intensity of color (in the colors for which they're designed) and a somewhat deeper tone than the deeptone bases.

3. Yellow Iron Oxide -- a very stable (weather and light-resistant) yellow with a red undertone.

4. Thalo Green -- a very stable green.

5. Thalo Blue -- a very stable blue.

6. Red Iron Oxide -- a very opaque brick red.

7. Exterior Yellow -- a nontoxic yellow with a red undertone -- now used to replace toxic medium chrome yellow.

8. Light Fast Red -- a clear, crimson (slightly wine-colored) red with a blue undertone.

9. Brown Iron Oxide -- a very opaque brown with a red undertone.

10. Calbizol Violet -- a stable violet.

11. Chromium Oxide -- a muted (dull) green with a yellow undertone.

12. Raw Umber -- a rather transparent earth brown.

Though it's simplest to choose one particular base for each color that you mix, any of the bases can also be combined with each other to achieve intermediate tone qualities.

Any of the colorants can be used in combination with each other to produce additional colors. But for a given quantity of paint, *never let the amount of colorant exceed 10 percent*. If you add more, there may not be enough binder in the base to hold the pigment to the wall once the paint dries.

It's important to note the undertones that some of these tints have. If a paint with, for example, a green undertone is painted over a large area, it may have a slight greenish cast. *Undertones are especially important for mixing*. It is well known, for example, that blue and yellow mix to make green. But if you mix thalo blue with yellow iron oxide (which has a red undertone), the red undertone will tend to muddy the green. However, thalo blue with hansa yellow (which has a green undertone) will be OK.

REMEMBER: Whether you are buying your paints ready-mixed or mixing them yourself, make sure that all your paints are of the same type; for example, all interior semi-gloss, or all exterior flat.

ARTISTS' ACRYLIC PAINTS FOR MURALS

Most of the recent Mexican murals, as well as a small but growing number of U.S. murals, have been painted in what we would call "artists' acrylic paints" (noncommercial paints formulated especially for the artist) -- with very exciting results. Artists' acrylics, as distinguished from the many commercial acrylic house paints ("acrylic" is a general term for a plastic vehicle that is widely used in many commercial and artists' paints), can have many advantages for the mural painter as well

as some disadvantages. This section outlines these
advantages and disadvantages for the guidance of the
mural painter in making a choice of paint to use.

Advantages of Artists' Acrylic Paints

Artists' acrylics have purer, truer colors than do
commercial housepaints. This is a distinct advantage
for the mural painter primarily because it makes mixing a wide range of colors possible. In order to mix
two colors to make a third, you must have pure tones
to start with or the mixed color will tend to be
muddy.

Another advantage of the artists' acrylics is the
intensity of the color. Commercial paints contain
many added chemical substances (for washability,
resistance to scuffing, and a wide variety of other
properties) that artists' acrylics don't have and
don't need. The added chemicals in commercial paints
tend to a certain degree to dull their color, whereas
in artists' acrylics the pure pigment is allowed to
show through with little interference. Thus the
colors of artists' acrylics have a considerably richer
appearance when applied to the wall.

A third major advantage of artists' acrylic paint is
its extendability. In general, commercial paints cannot be extended (that is, there is no practical way of
adding more vehicle to the paint to make it cover a
larger surface area) because extender for commercial
paints is not readily available to the consumer. But
with artists' acrylics it is easy to add a clear substance called "medium" to the paint to make it go
further. Thus it is possible to make transparent
glazes that cover a very large area by the addition
of the relatively inexpensive medium to a very small
quantity of original paint. This process of extending
can, in certain cases, cut down the cost of a mural
considerably. For example, if you want to paint a
large area of light blue sky in a mural, you can
either buy a couple of gallons of light blue commercial paint, or buy a much smaller quantity of intense
blue artists' acrylic paint. Then mix the artists'
acrylic paint with medium to make a thin blue glaze,
and paint the glaze over a white background to achieve
the same light blue color. And with some very strong
pigments -- for example, carbon black -- it is possible to add enough of the cheaper medium to extend the
original black artists' acrylic paint a lot and still
have a strong black color -- since artists' acrylics
have a higher concentration of opaque pigment than do
most commercial paints.

Disadvantages of Artists' Acrylics

One big disadvantage of artists' acrylic paints is
their relatively high cost. They are expensive in any
case, and if you are painting on a rough brick wall
(which greatly increases the surface area that the
paint has to cover), the cost per size of the mural

is even more. The resources and/or purpose of your project may simply not justify the cost of this kind of paint.

Another problem with artists' acrylic paints is that most, as far as we know, *have not been formulated specifically for outdoor use.* Unlike commercial exterior housepaints, they do not have the many chemical additives that protect the pigments from fading under the sun's rays. Therefore, while some artists' acrylic colors that contain natural light-resistant pigments will not fade, other colors made from pigments that are not in themselves light resistant may fade in time.

Another important factor is that the acrylic binder is less resistant to weather than are some other binders. This makes little difference on masonry, but acrylic is *not recommended for exterior use on wood* since wood expands and contracts considerably outside, and the paint film will not hold up long.

The artist planning a mural project must weigh all of these factors before deciding on what kind of paint to use. In general, we would recommend the use of artists' acrylics if: (1) you can afford them; (2) you have a smooth, rather than rough, wall (one solution to this problem if you do have a brick wall is to prepare the wall with block filler -- see the paint chart, remarks under masonry wall preparation -- to make a smooth surface); and (3) you can make practical use of transparent glazes in your painting.

If you are planning to paint an outdoor mural in artists' acrylic paints, be sure to check with the manufacturer about the light-fast (nonfading) quality of the pigments in each color that you plan to use. Probably the best solution to the color-fading problem is to coat the finished mural with a clear solution acrylic containing ingredients that absorb ultra-violet light; this substance is produced by several paint manufacturers (see the paint chart, remarks under *Sealer*).

GLOSSARY OF PAINT AND WALL PREPARATION TERMS

Listed below are technical paint and wall preparation terms that we have used in this chapter and elsewhere in the manual. These terms are also commonly used in paint stores and on paint labels, and in general are terms that you will run across and should know about -- to help you in selecting and understanding paints and in relation to walls and wall preparation.

Paint -- a liquid product made up of pigments (coloring), a binder or other vehicle (substance that binds the pigments to the wall), other ingredients added for durability, light resistance, etc., and a thinner (solvent) of water, mineral spirits, or other volatile (evaporating) liquid. When applied to a surface, paint forms an opaque (nontransparent) and protective covering by drying to a tough, colored film.

Pigment -- a synthetic compound or earth substance that has the properties of intense color and opacity (nontransparency). Pigment is the coloring agent in paint. Produced as a solid, it is finely ground and (in commercial paints) mixed with oil or a synthetic plastic which acts as a vehicle or binder to hold the pigment to the wall.

Vehicle -- an ingredient in paint which forms the paint film that binds the pigment and other solid ingredients to the wall when the paint dries. In commercial housepaints, the vehicle is either oil or alkyd (in oil base paints). Or it can be a synthetic plastic such as acrylic or polyvinyl acrylic (in latex paints).

Solvent -- water or an organic compound such as mineral spirits or turpentine that acts as a thinner and is in, or can be added to, a paint. Solvent is a volatile liquid that evaporates from the paint as it dries, leaving the pigment and vehicle (binder or film-former) on the wall.

Latex -- a broad term describing paints that are thinned with water. Latex paints are the same as emulsion paints and are made with an acrylic, polyvinyl acrylic, or other synthetic vehicle (binder) suspended in water.

Oil -- a broad term referring to paints that are thinned with a solvent such as mineral spirits, naphtha, or turpentine. Oil paints are made with a vehicle (binder) of oil or alkyd.

Alkyd -- a type of hybrid oil (chemical combination of oil and other materials) vehicle (binder) used in many commercial paints, especially enamels. Alkyd paints are generally more durable than paints made with pure oil.

Enamel -- an oil or alkyd base paint that is formulated to have a high gloss and/or extreme durability.

Acrylic -- the name for a synthetic plastic compound that is used as the vehicle (binder) in many commercial latex (water-thinned) paints and in artists' acrylic paints.

Medium -- a gelled acrylic emulsion used for mixing with artists' acrylic paints to extend them or to make transparent glazes. It works in the same way that linseed oil does with artists' oil paints.

Gloss -- a term used to describe the property of light reflection (surface shine) in a paint. A gloss paint has a very high reflection of light from its surface.

Flat -- a term used to describe paint whose surface is very dull (has a very low reflection of light).

Semi-gloss -- a term used to describe a paint whose surface has a medium shine (light reflection). Semi-gloss paint is halfway in light reflective quality between flat and gloss paint.

Base -- an incomplete paint, usually containing very little pigment, that is designed to be mixed with small amounts of high-intensity colorant to produce a complete paint. There are a number of base types designed to produce pastel shades, deep shades, etc., and many different colors can be produced from any one base, depending on what colorants are added to it.

Colorant -- also called "tinting color." A liquid mixture of concentrated pigment that can be added to a base to produce a colored paint, or to a paint to change its color. Colorants are available in two basic types, *oil colors* and *universal colors*. Oil colors can be used only in oil or alkyd paints, but within the same brand, universal colors can be used in both oil paints and latex paints. *Colorants should be mixed only with bases of the same brand.*

Efflorescence -- a white, powdery chemical deposit found on the surface of many brick and other masonry walls. It is caused by the action of moisture within masonry walls. Efflorescence prevents paint from adhering to the wall and must be removed before painting. Although surface efflorescence is easily brushed off the wall, the wall must also be chemically treated with a solution of zinc sulfate to inhibit the continued surfacing of more efflorescence from deep inside the wall.

9 How to Paint the Wall/Cleanup

Though each artist/organizer and team will have their own way of working, here are a few general guidelines that should make the process of painting the mural easier and more efficient. (While we do talk mainly about painting with brushes, there are other means of applying paint: air compressor/spray gun, rollers, etc. One of these might be more desirable for your project.)

PUTTING UP THE DRAWING

The blow-up of the small sketch onto a large wall cannot involve a large number of people. Usually the artist/organizer and the core group will transfer the drawing to the wall. After the grid is on the wall:

- one or two team members should stand on the scaffolding to draw in the sketch.

- others should stand back with the sketch and direct the drawing on the wall. Stand as near as possible to where the public will see the mural. *This prevents distortion of the drawing*. The people drawing at the wall *cannot* see the wall well. They have a distorted view and need specific directions given from a distance.

- constantly step back from the wall to make sure your drawing has the right proportions. Check it out from all angles, especially the angle from which the most viewers will see the mural.
  (If you are working on a really bumpy wall, some of your lines may appear wavy from certain angles -- check this out, too.)

- the sketch blow-up can be put on the wall with carpenter's chalk or compressed charcoal. (But be careful -- once we worked for two weeks on a chalk blow-up, and a day of rain washed off all our work.)
  If you can handle it, try drawing in the blow-up in paint. A good procedure is to get parts of the sketch down in chalk and then go over the final chalk lines with paint. Two people working together with this method can get a lot done fast.
  Avoid using magic marker -- it can come right through the paint and it's a real pain to cover up.

- to make large curves, "rehearse" the stroke with your arm 2, 3, or 4 times to get a natural, flowing line; then make your line with paint or chalk.

- use a yardstick or a straight-edge board to get long, even, straight lines (see Chapter 21, "Helpful Hints").

FILLING IN THE PAINTING

- Some of the team members with little art experience will want to fill in the flat areas of color. This should be done under the direction of the artist/organizer or a core group member.

- others with more confidence in art can do shading, detail, and final outline.

- no matter what the skills of your team members, *try to give each member variety in his/her work.* This will break the monotony and give confidence to everyone. Give everyone a chance to participate in all aspects of the painting.

- don't complete some areas of the mural down to the last detail while leaving other areas barely sketched in. *Try to divide the work on the total mural into stages* (for example: outline drawing, flat areas of color, shading, and detail), and complete each stage over the whole wall before going on to the next. *Make assessments and adjustments at each stage.* There are two main reasons for this:

    1. you may realize, after a lot of work on one section, that certain forms are too small, or too large, to go with the rest of the mural.

    2. the color and light-and-dark contrasts in each section should work well with the color scheme of the whole mural -- and the final color scheme often evolves gradually during the painting process. Keep this in mind.

- at lunchtime or day's end, stand back a distance and see what was accomplished. Talk about plans for the next day.

- evaluations of progress should be based on a combination of aesthetics and content -- are they working *together* to form a totally strong, unified mural?

- when you reach the final touch-up stage of painting, you might consider working from the top down. That way you can avoid drips and further retouching on sections you've just finished.

PAINT HINTS AND CLEANUP

Proper painting procedure is essential for achieving best results in your mural. Keeping the work and storage areas clean shows respect for the community; it promotes good relations with the sponsor, the owner of the building, etc. And be sure to provide adequate clean-up facilities for your team members. If you're working with young kids, sending them home covered with paint is not good for relations with parents; it's inconsiderate.

- make sure all paints are thoroughly mixed.

- *read all warnings* and cautions on paint labels and follow them.

- if you are painting indoors, make sure there is *adequate ventilation*.

- if it's been raining, let the wall dry out thoroughly before painting.

- wash brushes soon after use and always after a day's work.

- don't let brushes sit in cans of water or paint thinner overnight. Brushes will weaken and become limp.

- large paint spills and speckled work areas can be avoided by the use of simple drop cloths and other precautions.

- put paint tops on tightly to avoid spilling and to keep a skin from forming on top of the paint.

- gather all supplies into a storage room or a corner of the work space at the end of the day. Don't leave paints and supplies scattered around.

- let drop cloths dry before folding up.

WARNING: Dispose of paint rags soaked in paint thinner. Don't let them collect. PAINT THINNER IS FLAMMABLE. With rags soaked in some paints and varnishes, spontaneous combustion is possible. Be careful.

- the paint thinner you use should be suggested by the store or other supplier from whom you get paints. Follow instructions for use.

- cover cans of paint not in use -- open cans of paint and scattered materials might invite defacement of the mural.

10　The Classroom Mural

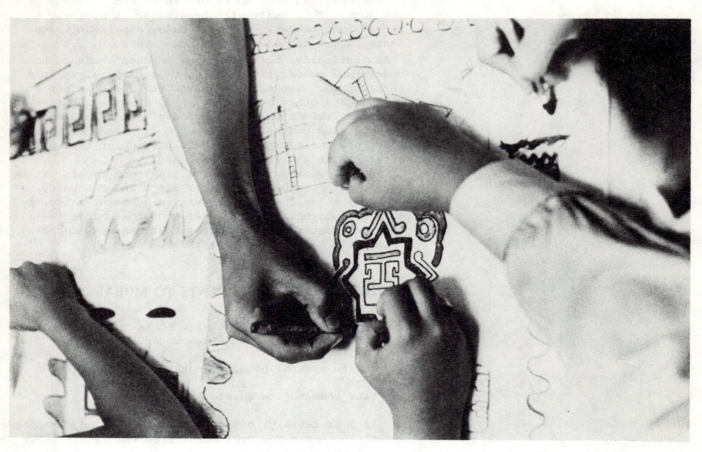

60.

The experiences gained through mural painting -- the process of discussion, planning, and collective creativity -- are an exceptional learning opportunity for students. Mural projects teach many skills at the same time, including social, as well as creative and technical. They teach responsibility to others, to the project, and to the public. Students learn about themselves through working with others. They also enjoy the sense of doing something for the people who will see the mural. Students will learn sensitivity to people by seeking a theme that will be meaningful to others.

In the process of doing a mural, the student, perhaps for the first time, will have a role in creating or changing his or her own environment. Murals enliven hallways, cafeterias, and other institutional areas, and a more humanized school environment is a benefit to everyone who enters the school.

A good mural project brings students together over a common topic. School art programs, to be most effective, need to be an organic part of the interests of the school and students. A mural project, then, cannot be just art for its own sake. It must relate to other parts of the school experience, such as social issues within the school, the culture and heri-

tage of the students, and/or subjects being studied.
For instance, the idea of a "mural through a microscope" can teach students to observe through a
microscope, and then to record these observations in
art form. The result will be greater involvement in
the subject matter. In every case, murals help students to see art as a living experience.

Aesthetically, mural painting teaches students to
understand color, line, and form as they relate to a
large space. Students learn how to handle paints and
brushes and other materials. They must decide together on selection, revision, evaluation, and choice
of color and composition. They must remember to consider how their expression of a particular idea will
affect those who will see the mural.

The following guidelines for classroom murals can be
used by art teachers in summer camps and community
centers, as well as by teachers in schools. Also, *be
sure to look throughout the rest of this manual* -- all
sections contain further ideas that can be incorporated into a classroom experience.

INTRODUCE YOUR STUDENTS TO MURAL PAINTING

- show them slides of murals, books on murals, and
  other available visual resources.

- invite a mural painter to talk to your class.

- take them to see murals in your area.

- if your library, city hall, train station, or post
  office has a New Deal mural from the 1930's, take
  a look at that.

- look at pictures of murals of the past, such as
  20th-century Mexican murals, Renaissance fresco
  paintings, etc. (See "Bibliography" at the end of
  this manual.)

GET TOGETHER A STUDENT MURAL TEAM

Teams gather somewhat naturally in a school setting.

- student teams can be formed in art classes, other
  classes, and student organizations. The art
  teacher should contact social studies, math, or
  other teachers and work with them.

- first, spark interest by having a small core group
  (4 or 5) of enthusiastic students do a small,
  simple mural (perhaps on paper, for a hall bulletin
  board).

- develop the mural where others can watch the progress.

- have the team sign a "mural group" list and keep
  it near the project for everyone to see.

- invite other interested students to join for a larger mural team.

- try to have workshops with parents, too -- so that they can be involved in the project, to work out ideas mutually.

- the first small mural may also get other teachers interested in using murals for their own class projects -- in social studies, languages, or whatever.

- the new mural team should get to know each other socially, at a party or over lunch.

WORK WITH THE TEAM IN DEVELOPING A THEME AND A SKETCH

With a classroom mural, maximum creative involvement of the team with the project is especially important because of the learning opportunities it gives.

- the teacher, as artist/organizer, is the promoter of discussion and should function to draw ideas out of the students. *Don't settle for the first idea expressed*, but keep encouraging and further developing the ideas.

    1. have students talk about themselves and the feelings and ideas they have in common. Give them time to think -- don't plunge right in trying to get final ideas.

    2. don't talk *at* the students if you expect to hear their ideas and to encourage their enthusiasm.

- have the students talk about the mural's surroundings and about the people who will see it.

- suggest possible themes to the students, such as family, neighborhood, historical situations, celebrations, current issues or crises, anything pertaining to class topics, the immediate feelings and problems of their age.

- the team can also meet with the student government, ethnic clubs, social issues clubs, and other student organizations to get ideas for a theme. They can ask friends and family, too.

- guide the students toward choosing a theme that their audience will relate to and that the whole team will get excited about. (See Chapter 5, "How to Develop a Theme.")

- base selection of the subject on the potential abilities and the maturity of the class. Interest in the subject can be furthered by an enthusiastic introduction by the teacher.

- when the theme is decided on, have each team member sketch his or her own ideas on how to put across the theme. (See Chapter 6, "How to Develop a Sketch.")

    1. have students make their sketches the same general shape as the wall.

    2. encourage students to go beyond trite ideas or clichés. The teacher should help them to produce their best efforts.

    3. don't throw any sketches away.

- select drawings with images that can be combined in a final sketch.

- select one drawing that has a basic design into which other ideas can be incorporated, and that has a style that will be easy for everyone to paint.

- *keep the basic design simple and clear enough for others not connected to the project to understand. Young people often try to take on more than they can handle.*

    1. the mural must fit well the space for which it is planned.

    2. keep in mind that the interest necessary to complete the project will have to be sustained over an extended period of time.

- when you're ready to do the mural, the team should decide on individual responsibilities for each team member.

    1. give everyone a chance to participate fully. Each member of the group should feel pride and a personal creative experience in the final product.

    2. be sure each student knows and understands what to do before work actually starts.

- it is important, especially with younger students, for the teacher to recognize successes throughout the project.

- when the mural is finished, the same team can stay together to do other more difficult and complex murals.

- team leaders could also direct their own mural projects with other students.

- carry on a continuous evaluation of progress. Discuss changes or additions as work progresses. As the mural nears completion, take extra time to consider it, instead of rushing to the finish.

TIME

Time is often a difficult factor in school situations.

- *keep the first project simple* so that it won't drag on for weeks. It's never good to let the project drag. A good idea is to set a completion date for a special event or school open house.

- if the students are enthusiastic enough about their mural, they will work extra hours on it -- lunchtimes and after school.

- you may be able to organize a summer project with your students when they will have more time.

- if you have a few students who are especially enthusiastic, you may want to put them in touch with other mural painters in the area who might want a few good assistants.

MESS AND CLEANUP

To minimize mess, take proper precautions.

- use newspapers or plastic or cloth drop cloths.

- tape the cloths to the floor and gather them up or push them against the wall at the end of each session.

- a strong soap or paint thinner will take up fresh paint quickly. It's *much* easier to clean up a spill right away.

- get a special basket or box to store paints and brushes -- maybe even a shopping cart.

- keep the work area clean. This will please school personnel and increase the possibility of mural projects in the future.

TYPES OF MURALS

Once the students are enthusiastic about doing a mural, there are many approaches open to the teacher. Probably the most exciting project would be to work directly on an indoor or outdoor wall, but in many schools this is not possible. Don't let this discourage you; less permanent murals can be a real asset, visually and in terms of content, to both the classroom and the general school environment. And remember, the *process* of doing a mural is a major aspect of the project and of the learning experience. Make use of whatever is around; adapt to what is available. Here are several alternatives:

61. Detail, mosaic on school

Mosaic Mural

A mosaic mural is made by mounting small objects, arranged to form patterns and pictures, on a board or other surface. It can be done with a variety of materials and is a particularly interesting medium for a classroom project.

- a great variety of small objects can be used as mosaic pieces: pieces of glass, small pieces of linoleum tile, bathroom tile, stones, pebbles, shells, macaroni, rice, dried beans, cut paper, buttons, and innumerable other found objects.

  1. colored glass can be collected outside. Different kinds of bottles provide a good range of colors. Other glass scraps can be obtained at little or no cost from factories that do glass work. *When breaking glass into smaller pieces, use a glass cutter,* not a hammer or your hand -- and *wear approved goggles.*

  2. defective linoleum tiles and bathroom tiles can be obtained from tile companies. To cut linoleum tile into smaller pieces, use heavy-duty scissors or a utility knife. Dipping linoleum in hot water will soften it for cutting.

- depending on the weight of the pieces, a number of different materials can be used as a surface on which to mount the mosaic: masonite, plywood, heavy cardboard, a bulletin board, or even the wall itself. For cut-paper mosaics, butcher paper may be used.

  To minimize warping of plywood or masonite, apply a base coat of clear lacquer to the board before mounting tiles.

- first, separate mosaic pieces into boxes by colors.

- draw the basic design on the board and glue the mosaic pieces in place.

  1. for lighter materials, use white liquid glue (like Elmer's Glue-All).

  2. for heavier materials (or for a mosaic that will be outdoors) use epoxy contact cement.

- for linoleum and bathroom tile mosaics, grout (a special cement filler available at ceramic supply stores) can be used to fill in the cracks between tiles and create a smooth surface.

62. Detail, mosaic mural on school playground wall

63. Mosaic mural in progress

64.

65.

Ceramic Mural

An ambitious and very exciting long-term project for students is a ceramic mural. This is a mural that can be made from a single slab of clay, designed as a whole and then cut into smaller sections for firing, glazing, and reassembly. (This is different from a mosaic mural, which is made by arranging small objects on a flat surface to form designs and pictures.)

A large kiln is necessary for such a project, but if your school does not have such a kiln, don't be discouraged. Firing for your project can also be done at a local ceramic center, a high school, or a community college. Also, ready-made ceramic tiles can be purchased at art or hobby stores and decorated by students. (For further information, see *Techniques* in "Bibliography.")

Doing a ceramic mural seems difficult, but with proper procedures work can go smoothly. It is very rewarding, especially for young children -- because clay is a three-dimensional medium that offers children the opportunity to work directly with their hands. It is a long-term project mainly because of the long periods of drying time required for the clay.

66. Detail, ceramic mural made by students

- the best kind of clay to use is *stoneware clay*, which is durable in all weather. (Be sure that you understand the qualities and types of clay before you begin the project.)

  For a 5' x 7' mural, at a 2" thickness (a good thickness for a mural), you will need about 500 pounds of clay.

- pack the clay into a wooden frame built from 2" x 2" boards to make a single flat slab.

  1. work on a large flat area, preferably in a damp location (like a basement) to keep the clay moist.

61

2. pack the clay into the frame by kneading and pounding. (Spend plenty of time kneading the clay to make sure that all the air is pressed out.)

- cover the clay with very moist heavy plastic (and wet rags at the edges) at the end of each work session.

- transfer your basic design into the clay slab, using one or more of the following techniques:

  1. coil -- modeling with rolled ropes of clay.

  2. slip -- liquid clay and water mixture (to which a pigment such as red iron oxide or cobalt has been added), which is brushed over the surface of the clay and than scratched into, revealing the color underneath.

  3. imprinting -- pressing objects into the clay to make marks or patterns.

  4. scratching.

  5. bas relief -- molding the surface of the clay into shapes.

- dry the clay slowly -- *the clay must dry slowly or it will crack.*

  1. for the first week of drying, keep the clay covered lightly with plastic, and with damp cloths at the edges.

  2. when the covering is removed, watch for cracks beginning to develop. If they do, re-cover the clay with a damp cloth.

  3. when the clay feels like hard leather (this takes about one month), it is ready for cutting.

- cut the clay into small sections (about 10" x 10") for firing.

  1. the slab may be cut into shapes -- like a jigsaw puzzle -- following the design, or in straight sections like a grid.

  2. before firing, number the backs of the pieces with a water solution of red iron oxide (a ceramic pigment that can be bought at any ceramic supply house).

- fire the clay *very slowly.*

  1. begin with a low temperature (100-200°) for 6 to 7 hours to ensure total drying.

  2. raise to medium temperature (400-500°) for 2 hours.

3. finally, gradually raise the kiln temperature to 1700° as in a normal bisque firing. Keep it at this temperature for about 4 hours.

- cool the clay very slowly. Remove the pieces from the kiln and reassemble the mural.

- glaze the pieces and refire at the temperature suitable to the recipe of the glaze you've used.

- attach the tiles to the wall with epoxy contact cement. (Although this is rather expensive, it is the best adhesive for walls.) Consult the school maintenance staff or a contractor to make sure that the wall on which you want to mount the mural can withstand the mural's weight.

- when tiles are mounted, fill in the spaces between **with** colored grout (a cement mixture specially made for this purpose).

Silhouette Mural

The silhouette mural is a quick and easy way to make a very exciting project. The description below can be adapted to *every* age group.

The silhouette mural involves using a light to cast shadows of figures on a background, and then tracing the shadows to make outlines of the figures, later to be filled in with paint. Many teachers have traced silhouette portraits of their students' faces in this way. The silhouette mural carries the technique one step further. All you need for this project is enthusiasm and a steady hand!

The silhouette mural is ideal for a first mural project because it is simple, quick to do, spontaneous, and fun. Students like to pose each other and try to capture the feeling they want, and there is much laughter and teasing. This technique also helps students understand their own shapes and sizes. The project ends in good feeling because the overlays of silhouettes look very nice. Silhouette murals are especially good for students who are shy about drawing, since *no drawing skills are needed to make the silhouettes look realistic and professional.*

67. Silhouette mural in progress

- use a focused light, like the light from a slide projector or a tensor lamp (a small, inexpensive reading lamp that uses a special high-intensity bulb), to cast shadows of the figures on the mural surface -- paper, cloth, or wall.

- have students experiment with posing in front of the light and gesturing and play-acting to express feelings. Have them watch the shadows to see that the feeling they are trying to express comes through in the silhouettes. Let them get comfortable with the technique.

- experiment with variations in heights and sizes of figures.

  1. position people at different distances from the light to get variations in size of the figures. A figure closer to the light will be larger.

  2. use chairs, tables, or ladders to get figures at different heights.

  3. vary the angle of the light beam. If you direct the beam upward from the floor, you will get a large, looming figure on the mural surface.

- instead of having a person stand on their head, you can get an upside-down figure by tracing a silhouette on a piece of paper, then turning the paper upside-down.

- when you've decided on the final composition of the mural, pose one person at a time in his or her designated position, trace all the silhouettes, decide on a color scheme, and paint it in.

  1. make sure that the feelings or situation you want to get across are expressed in the silhouettes on the wall.

  2. use profiles wherever possible. Do a good tracing job, especially on faces and hands, so that everyone can recognize the actors.

  3. have two people trace at once to complete the silhouette quickly. The poser gets tired fast. (When tracing the face, it's a good idea to put a steadying hand on the poser's head.)

  4. paint in the silhouettes. When silhouettes overlap, you may want to paint the overlapped area in a different color.

Paper Mural

This is an easy classroom project that can also be developed for the hall, cafeteria, library, or elsewhere.

- measure the bulletin board, the space above the blackboard, or some other unused area, and cut heavy paper to fit -- brown butcher paper or a heavy white paper is fine.

68.

69. Drawing on a paper mural

• work on the paper either before or after attaching it to the wall with masking tape. Here are some possible methods.

   1. paint or draw directly on the paper.

   2. have each student draw a person, animal, or object to go with an agreed-upon theme, and cut them out. Paste them to the paper and paint in a background.

   3. do a collage with colored paper, pictures from magazines, cloth, yarn, etc.

Tracing with an Opaque Projector

Have your students choose a picture (or a creative combination of pictures!) from a magazine, newspaper, or book, or use photographs in which students have acted out scenes for their mural. Project the image on the wall or paper background with an opaque projector, and trace and paint it.

Triwall Room Divider

Triwall is three-layered corrugated cardboard easily made into strong durable furniture and other objects by simple and inexpensive hand tools. A free-standing room divider can be constructed out of Triwall. (See *Techniques* in "Bibliography.") Murals can be painted directly on both sides of the divider.

Mirror and Window Murals

   1. make a mural using a mirror as the background. This kind of mural is especially interesting because you must solve the problem of using the reflection as part of the mural itself. Sometimes old discarded mirrors can be found in school basements, junkyards, etc.

   2. very nice murals can be made on windows, using either thin water-base paint or thin cut paper in mosaic patterns. Both of these give an effect like stained glass.

Cloth Mural

Murals can be painted on canvas that's attached to a wall, or on free-hanging cloth -- a painted banner. (See Chapter 12, "How to Do a Mural on Cloth.")

Portable Panel Mural

A mural can be painted on one or more large panels of masonite or other board. The panels can be easily assembled and disassembled, and the mural can be moved from place to place or hung permanently on a wall. (See Chapter 11, "How to Do a Portable Mural.")

71. Designing and painting the panels in the classroom

70. Installing the panels

72. A new mural for the cafeteria

11 How to Do a Portable Mural

Portable murals open up a new dimension in mural making. Painted on panels that can be easily put together and taken apart, portable murals can be painted in a studio (or any large room) and then transported in a station wagon or van from place to place for display.

Portable murals are especially suitable for specific topical subjects -- day-to-day political and social developments and such subjects as political campaign issues and voter registration. For emergency situations, and in response to crises, portable murals can be painted very rapidly. In a matter of days they can be out on display to raise, dramatize, and clarify issues -- at community centers, shopping centers, rallies, housing projects, and other gathering places. In addition, murals on more general subjects can be displayed in churches, child care and community centers, and clinics on a rotating basis.

Portable panels can also be adapted for display in one location. They can be painted and then attached permanently to an indoor or outdoor wall. (See end of this chapter.)

This chapter deals only with the technical aspects of making portable murals. See other sections of the manual for procedure on developing theme, sketch, team, etc.

73. 4-panel mural in progress, "Vote Your Future," Chicago

74.

PANELS

Consider the factors of weight and durability when you choose your panels. If your portable mural is to be permanently installed, the weight of the panels is of less importance. But if the panels will be continually moved around, weight is a major concern. Similarly, murals to be displayed outdoors will have to be built of more durable material than those to be displayed indoors. Some panel materials are easier to cut, each has a different weight, some are more porous than others, etc. Most suitable panels come in 4' x 8' size, and if desired can be cut down by the lumberyard.

● for outdoor murals, tempered Masonite is best ("tempered" means chemically treated for hardening and resistance to weather elements). We suggest 1/4" or thicker tempered Masonite or similar hardboard or a panel called "panel siding."

● for indoor murals, we suggest untempered Masonite. Use 1/8" panels if you plan to be moving the mural much -- 1/4" is very heavy. Upson board, a compressed cardboard product, may also be used.

● if you use 4' x 8' panels, it's a good idea to trim from 1 to 2 inches from one long side and from one end of each panel to make transportation easier. (See special suggestions later in this chapter.)

Construction

● build a frame backing for each panel.
   If the panel has one rough and one smooth side, you have the option of painting on either side. (Masonite or hardboard panels are sometimes available with one rough side and one smooth side or with two smooth sides.) This, of course, will determine on which side you attach your framing, or backing. If you decide to paint on the rough side, the mural will require more paint and will have a textured finish.

   1. use "1-by-2" lumber. ("1-by-2" describes lumber or boards 1 inch thick by 2 inches wide, coming in 8', 10', or longer lengths. Actually, a 1-by-2 nowadays is typically 3/4" x 1 3/4".)
      Grades of lumber and their prices vary greatly. "Furring grade" is usually sold by the bundle for as little as 4¢ per foot, but includes warped, knotty, and uneven boards. "Clear" or "screen stock" 1-by-2s, which may sell for 12¢ per foot and up, are knot free and usually quite straight and even. If you can afford it, use the more expensive or "clear" material.

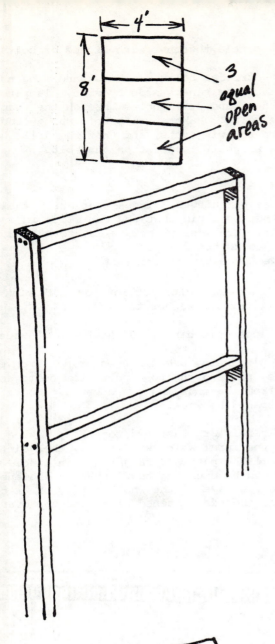

3 equal open areas

2. build a frame of 1-by-2 boards to be nailed to the back of each panel. The frame should be the same size as the panel, and, in addition, there should be two cross-pieces spanning the width of the frame -- equally spaced to make three equal open areas.

3. for a 4' x 8' panel, you will need two 8' (96") lengths of 1-by-2 for the sides, and four 3' 10 1/2" (46 1/2") lengths of 1-by-2 for the top, bottom, and two intermediate members. (If you've trimmed your panels down, have the lengths of your 1-by-2s correspond to the trimmed-down size of the panels.)

4. construct the frame so that the 1" (or narrow) edge of your lumber will rest against the panel.

5. join the frame together with "6-penny coated nails" (a nail about 2" long). Use two nails at each place where the 1-by-2s meet.

6. put triangular "glue blocks" inside each corner of the frame to brace it, if the mural is going to be transported often. Make glue blocks by cutting a 3" x 3" square of wood in half diagonally -- this makes two. Glue the blocks in place with ample exterior grade glue, and secure them with small brads or nails.

7. do all nailing on a flat surface to ensure that the frame will be flat.

8. nail the panel to the frame with 1" Masonite or hardened nails -- headless nails that are especially tough or tempered. Most ordinary nails will bend when hammered into Masonite. Place nails 6" to 8" apart.

9. constantly check to see that the panels lie perfectly flat against their frames, with no warping.

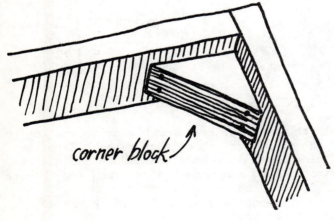

corner block

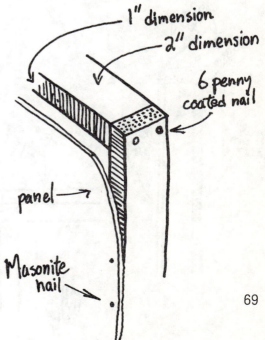

1" dimension

2" dimension

6 penny coated nail

panel

Masonite nail

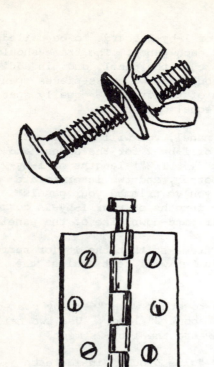

• join the panels together with hinges or bolts.

  1. use carriage bolts, washers, and wing nuts.
     (Place the panels side by side, clamp to-
     gether, and drill holes through the frame for
     the bolts. Make sure there's enough room to
     turn the wing nuts, and that the drill holes
     are slightly larger than the bolts.)

                     OR

     loose-pin hinges (hinges that are joined to-
     gether by a pin that you can slide in and
     out). Use screws, not nails, to attach the
     hinges to the frame.
       We suggest these sizes:

        carriage bolt: 2" long by 1/4" with wing
          nut and washer to fit

        loose-pin hinge: 3" high and 2" wide

  2. for 8' panels, use 4 hinges or bolts on each
     side, placing the top and bottom bolts about
     8" from the ends and the other two bolts even-
     ly spaced between.

• when the panels are fastened together, make a top
  edge for the mural which will steady the joints,
  keeping all the panels straight and in line. This
  top edge can be one long board that is fastened
  along the top edge of the whole mural, or it can be
  two or more boards fastened along the top over the
  joints.

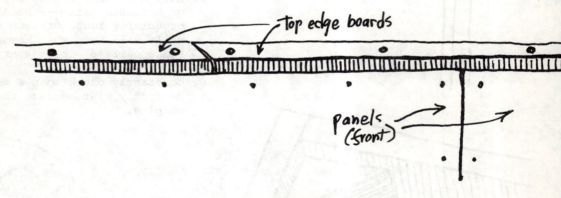

  1. use 1" x 3" board or boards.

  2. bolt the top edge board or boards to the top
     of the frame backing of each panel. Have the
     3" side of the top edge board down against the
     frame backing and the 1" side flush (even) with
     the front of the panels.
      use wing-nuts and bolts to attach the top
     edge to the frame.
      if you are using more than one top edge
     board, make sure each joint is well overlap-
     ped -- by at least 18" if you are using 4'
     panels.

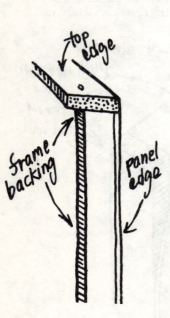

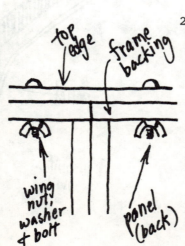

place bolts approximately 5" from either side of each joint. If you are using more than one top edge board, place additional bolts approximately 2" from the end of each board.

Painting the Mural

- if you are going to paint on the smooth side of the panels, sand them to roughen the surface slightly for better paint adhesion.

- after painting, seal both sides (and all edges) of the panels with clear varnish or sealer for weatherproofing. (See Chapter 8, "Paints and Wall Preparation" -- *Paint Chart*.)

Transportation and Installation

- before taking apart the mural for transportation, label all panels on the back in large letters and numbers.

  1. label each panel as to top/bottom.

  2. number all panels in sequence so that it will be clear which panel goes next to which.

- write out exact installation instructions on the back of one of the panels. The instructions should be simple enough so that anyone can put the mural together easily and safely.

- most portable murals can fit inside a large station wagon or van or can be tied to the roof of a car.

- when transporting the mural, cover each of the panels with a cloth or plastic fitted sheet, or place sheets between the panels -- to avoid scratching the paint and damaging the corners of the panels.

- make sure that all bolts, wing nuts, hinge pins, etc. are transported with the mural. To avoid losing them in transit, drill a series of holes in one of the cross pieces of the panel frame, where the bolts can be attached and stored.

- always bring along nails, wire, hammer, etc. when you go to install the mural. Usually you don't know in advance exactly where the mural will be placed and what materials will be required for installation. Also, you can't count on having these tools and supplies available at the place where the mural will be installed.

SPECIAL SUGGESTION: We suggest trimming 1 to 2 inches off one of the long sides of each 4' x 8' panel, and 1 to 2 inches from one end of the panel. This will make transportation easier since (among other reasons):

1. panels that are just under four feet fit flat on the floor of most large station wagons.

2. trimming the panels will make packaging the mural easier if you ever have to ship the mural. Crating materials (wood, cardboard, etc.) come in standard 4-foot widths; if you build a box that is 4 feet wide, your panels will have to be slightly smaller to fit in.

- if you have a clear space in front of the wall where the mural will be displayed, the easiest thing is to assemble the mural face down on the floor. (But *be sure* the floor is clean, so you won't damage the paint surface.)

- lay the panels face down (artwork down) and assemble. Don't forget to attach the top edge. Place the panels so that the bottom edge of the mural is about 1 foot from the wall. Then you can simply lift the top edge of the mural up and lean it against the wall.

- 4 or more people should help you lift the mural.

- lift the mural all at once, slowly and evenly, to prevent buckling.

- most portable murals are heavy enough so that you can simply lean the mural against the wall.

- for security, try to locate the mural near an object on the wall that it can be tied to. Drill holes in the frame backing near top and bottom to be used to tie or brace the mural to objects on the wall -- use wire or cord.

PERMANENT MURALS MADE ON PORTABLE PANELS

This type of project can be very useful if you have a wall that is difficult to reach or in too bad a condition to paint on directly, or if it's cold weather and you want to make a mural to go outdoors. The mural can be painted on panels in a classroom or studio and than mounted permanently on a wall.

- use 1/4" or thicker Masonite or similar hardboard material or panel siding for your panels.

    1. to stop the penetration of weather into the panels, seal the back and edges of all panels with a varnish or exterior latex primer. Prime the front side (before painting) with exterior latex primer.

    2. paint as you would an exterior wood wall. (See *Paint Chart* in Chapter 8, "Paints and Wall Preparation.")

- build a flat wooden framework or grid on which to mount the panels. The grid will first be attached directly to the wall, and then the panels attached to the grid. The special fasteners needed to attach the mural to the wall will splinter the paint if you put them through the panels. (This is also the reason why you should not try to attach your panels directly to the wall without a framework.)

75. Painting the mural panels in the classroom

IMPORTANT: This must be done in two steps, as described.

NOTE: For panels ½″ thick or thicker, the grid boards need be only at the edges of the panels, with no intermediate supports. For thinner panels we recommend adding an additional cross-piece for each panel. Thus, if you have 4′ x 8′ panels, your grid will be made up of 4′ x 4′ squares.

76. Fire department helps install the panels

77.

78. Dedication of mural, "Bored of Education," Chicago

1. for wooden walls, make the grid of 1 x 4 or
   2 x 4 lumber, depending on the condition of
   the wall and the weight of the panels.

2. for masonry walls (brick, concrete block,
   etc.), make the grid of 3/4" exterior plywood
   rippings (plywood strips about 4" wide). For
   interior masonry walls, you can use furring
   grade 1 x 3 or 1 x 4 lumber.

- attach the grid to the wall.

  1. for wooden walls, use coated nails or
     sinkers.

  2. for masonry walls that are new or in good
     repair, use 8 penny cut nails or other
     masonry nails. On brick walls, the nails
     should go into the mortar.

  3. for older masonry walls, it may be necessary
     to use ram-set or gun-fired fasteners. *We
     strongly recommend expert advice on the use
     of these devices -- THEY ARE DANGEROUS.*

- nail or screw the panels to the grid. We recommend that you use nonrusting nails and screws --
  galvanized nails and brass or aluminum screws.
  (Iron or steel nails or screws will rust and dis-
  color your mural.)

  1. with thin panels, space the nails about 8"
     apart.

  2. with thick panels, space the nails 12"-18"
     apart.

- We recommend making a weather seal at the top of
  the mural to keep water from getting behind the
  panels. (When water freezes in cold weather it
  can be very destructive -- ice expands with
  tremendous force and can buckle and possibly dis-
  lodge the panels from the grid.)

  Nail a piece of wood along the top of the mural.
  have it meet the wall (and caulk it to the wall)
  and slant down for water to run off.

74

12   How to Do a Mural on Cloth

Instead of painting directly on an indoor wall, you can do a mural on canvas with very good results. The canvas can be either glued directly to a wall or stretched on a frame that is attached to the wall. The first of these methods was used extensively by New Deal artists of the 1930s, and both can be very effectively used today. They will allow you most of the advantages of painting directly on a wall, plus other advantages -- one of which is that, handled properly, the painting can be removed from the wall. Another, less permanent, type of cloth project is the free-hanging painted banner, which can be quickly executed and easily moved from location to location.

MURAL ON CANVAS

It is preferable to paint this kind of mural after the canvas has been attached to the wall. Sometimes, however, this is impossible -- if the paint fumes will create an unhealthy atmosphere, for example, or if painting will interfere with other activities going on in the room.

The following are directions for making a mural in which the canvas is glued directly to the wall.

- measure the wall accurately.

- purchase canvas in dimensions larger than the measurements indicate, to allow for shrinkage (due to the liquid adhesive used in attaching the canvas to the wall).

- cloth for the wall can range from cotton duck canvas to linen, including heavy-weave linens. All of these come with either raw or already primed surfaces. Canvas in large dimensions suitable for murals can be bought at some art supply dealers and at places that sell canvas for theater scenery. (Ask at a theater and see where they purchase canvas for their theater flats.)

- repair the wall before attaching the canvas so that you have an even surface. Make certain that the wall is clean and greaseless -- remove wallpaper.

- consult an expert wallpaper hanger about the adhesive to use in gluing the canvas to the wall. The adhesives are usually water based, but the formulas can vary depending both on the canvas used and on the type of wall.

- try to get professional help (from a wallpaper hanger) on the installation of the canvas. Bubbles can form under the cloth. Seams in the cloth and working around architectural features like doors can also pose problems.

NOTE: Consideration should be given to the type of paint used and the effects of the ingredients of the adhesive on it. When acrylic paints are used, the acrylic gel medium is recommended as an adhesive.

- when canvas is glued to the wall, prepare the canvas surface with several coats of gesso or acrylic medium.

- we recommend painting the mural with either artists' oil paints or artists' acrylics.

If you want to paint on the cloth before installing the mural, work with the canvas tacked tightly against a wall or lying on the floor. Because you won't know the exact amount of shrinkage when the canvas is installed, paint beyond the calculated dimensions of the wall. Be extremely careful when attaching the already painted canvas to the wall. If possible, call in an expert to help.

The alternative method of attaching the canvas to a framework on the wall is useful if you have a very irregular or broken wall that cannot be repaired.

- build a secure frame of 1 x 2 boards around the edges of the area you want to paint.

- cut the canvas a little larger than the dimensions of the area for the mural.

- position people at the center of the top, left, right, and bottom sides of the frame to stretch the canvas. Securely fasten the canvas with nails or heavy-duty staples at the top center of the frame. Do the same with the right, left, and bottom sides. Move slowly around the entire frame, stretching and fastening tightly and evenly.

PAINTED BANNER

This type of project is often seen in churches and schools. It is a piece of cloth, painted or otherwise decorated, that hangs against a wall or hangs free in a room.

- both sides of the cloth can be decorated.

- a variety of materials can be used to decorate the banner: paints, pieces of felt (glued or sewn on), buttons, yarn, or thread, etc.

- if you want the banner to hang straight and stiff, attach light wooden poles or dowels along the top and bottom edges of the cloth. Tack the poles to the cloth, or sew folds in the top and bottom edges of the cloth to slide the pole through, like a curtain rod.

13   Other Techniques/Durability

We have talked mainly about painted murals because
generally paints are the cheapest and easiest material
to use. Many other materials, such as tile, mosaic,
stained glass, and fresco, would make the cost of the
mural possibly 2 to 10 times as great and would require special expertise because of their technical
difficulty.

Some of these techniques can be much more permanent
than paint. In Mexico, most of the outdoor murals are
in tile, mosaic, or stone, all of which can withstand
weather better than paint. Fresco painting is mainly
used on indoor murals or outdoors under balconies,
and is also very durable since the pigment is in the
plaster of the wall, not just on the surface. In the
"Bibliography" we have indicated some books that will
help you with techniques, procedures, and equipment
when working in other media. Your local library
should have some of these and other helpful books.

Permanence in murals depends on many elements: the
durability/quality of the medium (paints, tiles,
etc.), good wall preparation, state of the wall surface the medium is applied to, and upkeep of the
work. A mural painted with "cheap paints," if indoors and well kept up, can remain for a long time.
On the other hand, even murals done with first-rate
materials are subject to damage. Even a tile mural,
if it's outdoors, needs to be mended occasionally. No
medium will stand up well on a wall of a building
affected by poor roof drainage.

Investigate the wide variety of media that are po-
tentially available to the mural painter. Look at
techniques that have been developed by muralists of
the past in the United States, Mexico, and elsewhere -- fresco, encaustic, oils, pyroxylin, acrylics, and other media -- and think about how they can
be useful to us today. Many materials used for commercial purposes and industry can and are being adapted well for murals: porcelain enamel, enamel on
copper, scraffito, ceramic, tile and mosaic, brick,
vacuum molding with acrylic sheeting, and other media.

As far as paints are concerned, there are superior
paints available -- some of which we may not even know
of, should be investigated. Even though many muralists will probably not be able to afford the very
best paint products, still a thorough investigation of
the paint field should be made so we can obtain the
best products available within our price range. Cli-
matic considerations will allow one paint to be excellent in one place and not in another. Chemicals
and other pollutants in the air affect the media
differently from one place to another.

We must also secure newer and better walls -- get
in touch with architects and planners and have our
murals included as part of the original plan for new
housing projects, clinics, and other buildings. In
Chapter 18, "Scaffolding," we mention advanced

scaffolding rigs that could be useful to the muralist. Projectors of all sorts, cameras and special lenses can be useful; the air gun and other painting and spraying methods can be used. The whole territory of polychrome sculpture has been incorporated into murals by the Mexican muralist Siqueiros; he used pneumatic hammers, metal cutting and forming machines. New ways of working remain to be discovered. The purpose of investigating and/or using any of these materials is to produce works of art that better relate to the public.

79. The wall before work begins

80. The primer

14 Documentation

Make an effort to record the progress of your mural project at all stages, from the first sketches through the painting to the mural dedication. Documentation can serve many purposes. For yourself and the team, it's a good record of the different stages and struggles the project went through. It can be helpful to other artists who want to see how the mural was done. Photographs and other materials can be used for exhibits and publicity. Documentation is also an important permanent record of the mural. Unfortunately, many murals do not remain for years, because of peeling or fading, defacement, or even destruction of the wall.

Below are several specific suggestions for documentation -- take on what you can and involve others to make a more complete record of the project.

81. The team

82.

- save all sketches and reference material.

- try keeping a written diary: make a list of all the team members (with addresses and phone numbers), and record problems, progress, and complications from the selection of a wall through to the dedication.

- take photos of all stages of painting from the blank wall through to the dedication, including pictures of the team at work. For color slides outdoors, we recommend: High Speed Ektachrome (daylight). For black and white film indoors and outdoors, we recommend: Tri-X. We recommend that the film be processed by Kodak for good quality at a reasonable rate. (This is not an ad for Kodak; we haven't had very good luck with drugstore processing.)
  Color slides are very useful for slide talks. When projected, they are large and easy to see. Color and black and white prints can be made from color slides. Black and white pictures can be used for newspaper photos, exhibits, etc.

- have a team member tape record the comments of passers-by.

- make a complete photographic portrait of the finished mural. To portray the work itself, how it fits into the rest of the community, and how it fits visually with nearby buildings, be sure to include the following shots:

  1. shot from a distance. If you can't get far enough away from the mural to get it all into one shot with an ordinary lens, try using a wide-angle lens, 35 mm or 28 mm, to record the entire mural in a single photograph. This might distort the appearance of the mural, but the photo will still be a worthwhile document.

2. straight-on shot of the whole mural.

3. angle shots of the whole mural from left and right sides.

4. several close-up shots of details of the mural.

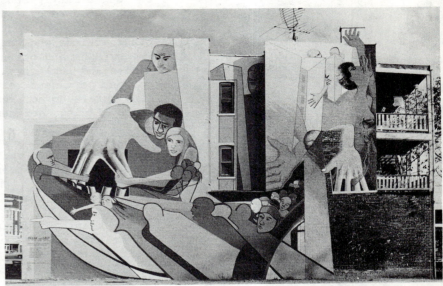

83. The completed mural, "Break the Grip of the Absentee Landlord," Chicago.

84.

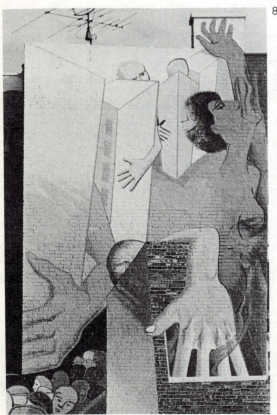

15   Dedication

The mural dedication is held to celebrate the fin-
ishing of the mural and to officially turn it over
from the team to the entire community. Usually the
dedication will be an event taking place in front of
the mural with refreshments, speeches, picture taking, and music. It is a very important event, especially for the team.

85. Dedication with the community,
"For a New World," Chicago

PUBLICITY

Even before the completion of the mural, consider
generating publicity through local papers, leaflets,
and other means. Publicity throughout the entire
project can increase community interest and help bring
in financial support.

• put out a leaflet (in all languages of the community) inviting people to the dedication. Include:
    place
    date
    time
    description of activities
    a short description of the mural project
    artists
    sponsors

• put out a press release and/or information packet.

Make up a one- or two-page typewritten document
giving the vital information on the mural. Include
a photo if possible. Mention:

86. She's a community resident and
    helps to dedicate the mural,
    "Let a People Loving Freedom,
    Come to Growth," New York

87. A jazz dedication, "The Philosophy
    of the Spiritual," Chicago

88. Songs celebrate "Protect the Peoples' Homes," Chicago

```
location
size
techniques
title
subject/theme
who worked on it
who sponsored it
how long it took
```

Mail it to the press and/or to people and organizations who would be interested in the project and who might help publicize the dedication.

THE PLAQUE

● paint a plaque on or beside the mural, giving:

```
title
date of completion
names of artist/organizer and team
names of sponsors, supporters, contributors of
   supplies, etc.
copyright notice, if there is one.  (See Chapter
20, "Copyright.")
```

THE DEDICATION CAN BE A STREET FESTIVAL

● have speakers -- parents of the team, team members, community organizers, civic leaders, other artists -- to speak about the mural, the issues it raises, and its relation to the community.

● serve refreshments.

● invite community musicians or talent groups to provide entertainment.

● invite community leaders.

GET THE COMMUNITY TO CONTRIBUTE

● ask community residents/stores to provide refreshments.

● request special community recognition for the team. Community organizations can make the mural team honorary members, for example.

16   Finances

The artist/organizer often has the major responsibility for fund raising for the mural project. The average cost of a mural on a two-story wall can run up to $200 or more for paints, brushes, scaffolding rental, insurance, etc., so you will probably need some kind of financial aid.

First, try to get a friend or organization to handle the fund raising for you. If you have to arrange for funding yourself, here are several possible sources:

LOCAL ORGANIZATIONS

Try to get a local organization or agency to fund the project. You might have to make up a written proposal before you approach some organizations: Here are some possibilities:

    chamber of commerce
    state or local arts council
    neighborhood organizations
    political organizations
    churches
    unions
    private donors

GRANTS AND DONATIONS

- look into applying for a large contribution or grant. (See *The Bread Game: A Guide to Foundation Fundraising*, or other similar publications.)

- some people and organizations will fund parts of the project or portions of the budget.

- you can divide your budget into $5-$25 chunks for small contributions.

SCHOOLS

- if you're a teacher, your school may fund the project. Look into special school funds set aside for public relations, building decoration or maintenance, clubs, student government, etc.

- if you're not a teacher, you may be able to get a school to fund or contribute to the project if its students are working as part of your team.

RAISING MONEY ON YOUR OWN

You can raise significant amounts of money here and there on your own, especially with community help. Keep a budget so you know how much you have to raise.

- Any and all of the following possibilities may be used, some more than once:

  > bake sales
  > art shows
  > rummage sales and garage sales
  > pay-at-the-door parties
  > amateur shows, concerts, theater

OTHER IDEAS

- ongoing publicity in local newspapers, radio talk shows, etc., throughout the entire project can help sustain interest in the wall and keep material and financial support coming in.

- instead of money, you can get people to donate supplies. (See Chapter 17, "How to Get Supplies.")

Remember, to get people to contribute money, you have to present the project as something that's good for the community.

talk about involvement of youth.

talk about issues the mural will raise.

talk about how the mural will improve the appearance of the community.

Whatever way funds are gotten, these matters are very important:

- an accurate accounting should be made of all funds received.

- regular receipts should be issued for all contributions made.

- a complete record of all finances will help you estimate the cost of future projects.

- thank-you letters should be sent to all donors expressing appreciation and encouraging their future help.

17 How to Get Supplies

Take a good look around the community you are working in. Often -- whether it be from door-to-door collections, contact with organizations, or contact with local businessmen -- most of the materials needed for your project can be gathered from the community. This process of gathering supplies can be very valuable in winning friends for the new mural -- it can help involve many others outside the day-to-day painting of the project. No door-to-door work is wasted effort. The main supporters and protectors of the mural will be the people living in the vicinity of the mural. If you do have to buy some of your supplies, look into good discounts.

CONTACT LOCAL BUSINESSES

- find out from neighborhood residents what businesses would be good to contact.

- try to get support of churches, clubs, community organizations, and even the local alderman before you approach the business.

- write a letter (preferably on your sponsor's or other friendly organization's stationery) to the public relations director of local paint companies, hardware stores, etc., describing your project. Include:

  location of the mural

  information about the neighborhood where your mural will be

  the mural's theme and how it relates to the community

  how the mural will help the whole community, with youth involvement, etc.

  your sponsors

  how much work has already been done, and how much money has already been contributed. You should make them feel that they are contributing to a solid project that is well underway -- a little more help from them will put you over the top!

  how enthusiastic you are about the project

  how much their help will be appreciated

  offer to mention them in the mural plaque or dedication ceremony, or give them credit in some other way a word about your own past experience

- if there's no response two weeks after sending the letter, call the company. Speak directly to the public relations person. This call will often get results, since they already know about the project from your letter.

DONATIONS

Try to get special supplies donated by the local hardware store. They may be willing to give you:

    cans of paint (possibly with torn labels or dents)
    brushes
    masking tape
    wire brushes
    paint hats
    mixing sticks

BORROW EQUIPMENT

Local schools, churches, colleges, union halls, and other organizations may lend supplies such as:

    ladders
    scaffolding
    an opaque projector

OTHER SOURCES

Local church groups and service organizations (like the PTA) can collect coffee cans, margarine tins, and other containers with lids for paints. These same groups can help provide meals and other refreshments for the team, or may help by organizing bake sales, etc.

If you can't get local help, get suggestions from artist friends and others about good places to apply for donations or discounts elsewhere in the area.

18   Scaffolding

Scaffolding is one of the more complicated aspects of large-scale mural painting. It's extremely useful, and for a large wall absolutely necessary, but it can also be expensive; and if it's abused can be very dangerous. It can also be a legal hassle. (See Chapter 19, "Insurance.") If you have a low wall, you can do very well with ladders (see *Ladders* later in this chapter), or even makeshift support like tables. But DON'T TAKE RISKS, even with these. (At the end of this chapter there is a section on advanced equipment used by sign painters, utility companies, etc. All of this equipment can have potential application to mural painting.) We cannot make specific recommendations for scaffolding, because we do not know the unique circumstances of your project. Contact experts for advice.

Still, the following information is important to know:

WARNING: Since we don't know the specific circumstances of your mural, we won't recommend a type of scaffolding.

RENTAL

Scaffolding rental can be expensive. Prices vary tremendously from area to area, but in large cities rental can run from $35 to $100 or more a month for 2-story scaffolding, including frames, wheels, jacks, and horizontal walking planks. Naturally, the price of scaffolding depends on the height of the wall, its length, and special equipment that might be required.

- some schools, churches, union halls, etc., own scaffolding, and may loan it to you, but insurance problems often make them hesitate. (See Chapter 19, "Insurance.")

- if you rent, explain your project in detail to the rental company. Let them suggest the type of scaffolding, how much to get, extras, etc. They have experience in handling many unique problems.

- a convenient type of scaffolding for many murals is called "rolling tower scaffolding." You can climb high on it and it can be moved from side to side. On the other hand, some muralists have used stationary scaffolding built in front of the entire surface of their wall.

WARNING: Avoid sign-painter's (hanging) scaffolding. Sign-painter's scaffolding is a horizontal planking suspended by ropes or cables anchored to the roof of the building. It is extremely dangerous and not recommended for most mural projects. (See Advanced Equipment at the end of this chapter.)

89. Team on a rolling tower scaffolding

- rent enough scaffolding so that you *don't* have to *take risks*.

- you are responsible if parts of rented scaffolding are stolen. Lock up scaffolding to post or fence at night.

SCAFFOLDING SAFETY TIPS

- obtain a detailed list of safety rules from the scaffolding rental company.

- have an expert (the rental company or an experienced contractor) put up the scaffolding.

- be careful with used scaffolding. Make sure it's in good condition.

- if the scaffolding is delivered the day before you put it up (or earlier), store it overnight by chaining the frames together and taking all the braces and small pieces (wheels, screw jacks, etc.) into someone's garage or apartment or some other safe place.

- fasten all braces securely before using scaffolding.

- lock the wheels (with casterbrakes) at all times except when moving scaffolding.

- legally, the height of rolling-tower scaffolding must not exceed four times the smallest dimension (width) of the base.

- don't use ladders or makeshift devices on top of scaffolding to increase the height.

- tie or lock top of scaffolding to the wall when leaving the mural site to prevent toppling from wind.

- For extra security attach a series of eye bolts along the upper part of your wall to tie or snaphook your scaffolding to. 1/4" or 5/16" eye bolts should be spaced from 8' to 10' apart. As you move your scaffolding along the wall, secure it to the nearest eye bolt. If you have a masonry wall, use a carbide bit drill. Insert an expansion nut such as Ackerman-Johnson into the hole (and set with correlating drive-set tool). Screw the eye bolt into the expansion nut. When the mural is finished, either unscrew or leave in the eye bolt.

- a warning sign should be attached near the bottom of the scaffolding to discourage people, especially kids, from climbing on it when the team is not working.

- enclose the entire base of the scaffolding with chicken wire or some other kind of fencing to keep people out at night.

- make sure scaffolding is straight up. Don't let it lean in any direction.

- if the scaffolding is resting on the earth, sand, etc., be sure that the foundation of the scaffolding is secure and will not sink into the surface because of the weight on it.

- make sure the ground under the scaffolding is level and solid. Rocky surfaces are very bad because they aren't level and because moving the scaffolding is difficult and risky. If it catches on a rock, it may topple.

- move the scaffolding slowly. Don't jerk it.

- 3 or 4 people are needed to move scaffolding safely.

- when moving, watch out for holes in the ground or floor, and also for overhead obstructions.

- no one should ever be on a scaffold while it is being moved.

- remove or secure materials and equipment on platforms before moving scaffolding.

- make a wide base of planks for standing on at each level.

- planking should overlap at least 6 inches over the edges of the scaffolding.

- put stops or cleats (little blocks or wood) on underside of the planks near the ends to keep planks from sliding off supports.

- make sure planks have little spring or bounce in them. This can be very wearing on the leg muscles over a long period of time.

- nail the planks together with 2-by-4s to keep them from getting ripped off -- they're expensive to replace. (The 2-by-2s can function as your cleats to prevent slippage.)

- remove planks or tie them down at night to keep them from blowing away. Even heavy wood or metal planks can blow away in a stiff wind.

- scaffolding is slippery on wet days.

- scaffolding is not a jungle gym. Caution and respect should be emphasized.

- no one should be on scaffolding except the mural team.

put cleats on both ends of plank!

WARNING: There may be legal and insurance hassles about kids 16 and under on scaffolding.

- no more than 3 people should be on any one level of scaffolding.

- rope up the "holes" in the scaffolding: put two or more safety ropes across each open section.

- climb up and down on the inside of the scaffolding.

- don't climb on diagonal (slanted) cross braces.

- use both hands for climbing.

- use a pulley to raise and lower supplies. Don't carry supplies while you climb.

- keep pulley ropes away from climbing area.

- keep one hand on bar of scaffolding while you paint with the other hand.

- don't reach far out from sides or top of scaffolding.

- don't scatter paint containers on walking planks. Keep them together.

- don't use the walking planks for a palette. Wipe up spills.

90.

LADDERS

Ladders can be very useful for painting on low walls (up to one story). The expense is much less (they can usually be borrowed), and they can be carried, put up, and removed easily each day. But they are more difficult to paint from, and there are definite safety risks with ladders. Contrary to what might be expected, they are actually less safe than properly used scaffolding, because of their relative instability. If you are going to use ladders, read the following carefully.

- you can use either step ladders (A-shaped ladders that stand on their own) or extension or other straight ladders (which lean against the wall).

  1. stepladders are better for use on hard surfaces like sidewalks。

  2. straight ladders are better for use on bare ground, where the bottom end of the ladder can sink into the ground a little.

- make sure ladders are in good condition. Don't use ladders with broken or loose rungs, and don't use a stepladder that doesn't have proper balance.

- make sure the ladder is steady and straight and on solid ground before you climb on it.

1. if you are working on bare ground, be sure that the ladder is not resting on broken glass or other debris or on rocks, and that the ground is even.

2. if you are working on a hard surface, be sure that the ladder will not slip out from under you. Some ladders are equipped with non-skid "shoes" for slippery surfaces.

- if you're using a straight ladder, try to tie the top of the ladder to something on the wall, or roof.

- straight ladders should lean against the wall at about a 70° angle.

- have two strong people move large ladders.

- the proper way to put up or take down long straight ladders is to "walk" them up and down. To walk a ladder up, lay the ladder on the ground, at right angles to the wall, with the bottom end nearer the wall. Have one person stand on the lowest rung of the ladder (or, if you are short of people, push the bottom end of the ladder right against the wall). Have another (strong) person "walk it up" -- lift the top rung over his or her head and then "walk," lifting rung by rung toward the wall. When the ladder is erect, pull out the bottom to the proper angle.
  To walk the ladder down, do the same thing in reverse.

- Do not ever "throw down" a ladder from the wall. A free-falling wooden ladder is extremely heavy and can severely injure someone -- and a sudden gust of wind can make a falling ladder land anywhere. Also, the fall may break the ladder.

- when painting on any kind of ladder, always lean into the ladder; don't lean back or overreach.

- use a paint hook to hang your paint can from a rung of the ladder while you work.

- if it's windy, don't use high ladders.

- if you plan to be off the ladder for any period of time, take the ladder down.

- if you are using straight ladders, look into using ladder jacks to rig up a working platform between two ladders. A ladder jack is a heavy metal brace that hangs from a ladder and provides a level surface on which the end of a wooden platform ("walker raft") can rest.

1. have an experienced painter, roofer, or handy-man show you how to use the jacks properly.

2. always make sure that the jacks are properly attached to the ladders, and that the platform is level before allowing anyone onto the platform.

3. no more than two people should be on the platform at a time.

4. sit (don't stand) on the platform, and don't lean back!

ADVANCED EQUIPMENT

For most community mural projects, the following equipment is probably not appropriate, either because of the danger involved or the high cost, or both. But since such aids have been used by muralists, and in some cases will be necessary in extraordinary mural projects, we list below some of the advanced equipment that is available. For projects involving younger people, we do not recommend any of this equipment.

• *hanging scaffolding* (also known as "sign-painters' scaffolding," and "swing-stage") is a horizontal planking platform suspended by ropes or cables anchored to the roof of the building. The height is adjusted by a pulley system on the ropes, or by the operation of electrical or air powered machinery. Safety lines are necessary at all times.

1. do not use hanging scaffolding on a team project. Hanging scaffolding is extremely dangerous because a single faulty part or a slip in operating could be fatal. In some places, a special insurance bond is required before using such scaffolding. The scaffolding holds a two-person load.

2. hanging scaffolding is most useful on buildings that are too high for use of regular scaffolding, but it is expensive, and the working platform is not wide enough to allow you to stand back and look at the painting. Unless you have a powered stage, it is hard to raise and lower.

• *bosun chair* is a one-person, seat-shaped chair which operates like hanging scaffolding. It might be useful for touch-up or repair work, but the range on the wall is limited to one vertical line.

• *cherry picker* is at the end of a boom mounted on a truck and carries one or two people. It is used by utility companies to repair street lights, signs, etc.

91.

● *mobile platform* operates from the back of a truck
and provides a stable, relatively large working
area. The movement of the platform can be con-
trolled by the person standing on it.

92.

19 Insurance

This chapter is concerned with the risks you face due to liabilities for injury to other persons and for damage to their property. The extraordinary hazards inherent in mural painting, particularly where scaffolding is involved, make adequate insurance coverage of your operation a necessity. One should aim at insuring any persons concerned with the project, including the team, sponsors, building owner, etc. If a suit should be brought against you for damages, the insurance company will represent you in court; if you are found by the court to be liable, the insurance company should pay your damages. The risks of liability are great, and insurance is your only protection.

We are not experts on either insurance or the law. All we can do here is give a general outline of the insurance situation and suggest some ways to begin dealing with it. For essential details about your rights and liabilities as director of a mural project, you will have to consult a lawyer. For comprehensive guidance on insuring your unique project, you will have to consult a good insurance broker.

SCAFFOLDING ACT

Before you get insurance of any kind, read the Scaffolding Act in your state. (To get hold of this, start by calling your city hall.) A Scaffolding Act generally imposes strict liability on people engaged in scaffolding operations. Reading the Scaffolding Act will tell you what is mandatory under the law in terms of insurance, structural requirements, age limits, etc.

TYPES OF INSURANCE

There are two main types of insurance that you will probably need for your project to be fully covered. The first is *public liability insurance*. The second is *Workmen's Compensation Insurance*.

Public Liability Insurance

- a public liability policy generally covers two areas: *bodily injury* and *property damage*. The policy covers these damages when they are suffered by members of the public (that is, people *not* working on the project) as a result of your mural activity.

  1. bodily injury to a member of the public can result if a can of paint or a piece of equipment falls on someone, if someone slips and falls on a paint spill, if scaffolding falls on someone, or similar curcumstance.

For bodily injury, look into a policy specifying "minimum limits of $100,000/$300/000." This means that the insurance company will pay up to $100,000 damages per person and up to $300,000 for injuries involving more than one person.

2. property damage can occur if a can of paint falls on an automobile, if paint damages the clothing of a passer-by, if paint splatters on a building, or similar circumstance.

   For property damage, look into a policy specifying a "minimum limit" of $50,000 for payment on property damage liability.

Public liability policies are generally of two types: *schedule* and *comprehensive liability* policies. A schedule policy provides liability insurance for certain risks specifically selected by the insured in an attempt to tailor the policy to his or her operations. The insurance company will not assume your liability if they determine the injury results from a cause outside of the schedule of insured risks. A comprehensive liability policy by its nature provides coverage for a wider spectrum of insurable liability hazards. Because of the difficulty of predicting the many different risks involved in a mural operation, the comprehensive policy offers greater protection. Even under a comprehensive liability policy, however, it is important that you explain fully to your insurance agent the nature of activities you will be engaging in, and secure the agent's commitment to take on the job.

Workmen's Compensation Insurance

• Workmen's Compensation Insurance will protect you in case of suits arising from injury to people working on the project.

1. by law, the employer is required to carry Workmen's Compensation Insurance for his or her employees. This means that if you, or your sponsor, are paying your team members to work on the mural project, you must get Workmen's Compensation Insurance for them.

2. related to Workmen's Compensation Insurance is Employer's Liability Insurance, which provides coverage for injuries suffered by your employees for which you are liable beyond the limits of the State Workmen's Compensation Law. Every Workmen's Compensation policy automatically provides coverage for Employer's Liability.

3. even if the team is all volunteer, you may well be liable if any team member is injured. This is a "gray area" that you should go over with a lawyer in relation to your project.

You may find it necessary to buy Workmen's Compensation or some other type of insurance to cover volunteer workers.

There are many "gray areas" of uncertainty that will have to be worked out specifically with a lawyer and an insurance broker -- and that will vary according to the unique circumstances of your project, such as: Who on the project will be the holder of the insurance policy? What are the state requirements for scaffolding liability? Do the team members meet the qualifications of "employees," and if not, how can they be insured?

WAYS TO GET INSURANCE

- ask your sponsor -- school, church, community organization, etc. -- to have your project included under their insurance coverage. Make certain their policy is adequate to cover the special requirements of the project.

- see if the owner of the building will provide protection on a short-term basis for the specific project. Speak directly to the insurance broker who covers the building to make sure that the policy is adequate.

- ask an insurance broker about short-term insurance for the time needed to complete the project. Describe your project in detail.

SUPPLEMENTS TO INSURANCE

There are several ways in which you can attempt by contract with the persons and businesses you will be involved with to limit your potential liability for damages. These contractual arrangements are not an alternative to insurance, but merely a supplement to insurance in order to reduce the possibility of liability.

Hold Harmless Insurance

- When a building owner or landlord permits you or hires you to paint a mural on his or her property, you should try to reach a written agreement to release you or "hold you harmless" for damage to the property. If the building owner will not agree to hold you entirely harmless, you may still be able to limit your liability to a fair amount.

Release Form

- Mimeograph, on sponsor's stationery if possible, a large number of "release forms" to be signed by

REMEMBER: This is only an approximate guideline.

97

WARNING: Remember that in most cases this will be only a "gentlemen's agreement," a moral deterrent to a potential suit, not a substitute for insurance.

WARNING: Each project is unique, so word the release form to fit your project. Have parents sign for team members 17 and under.

all team members. If this form is correctly worded, it could be legally binding. Have a lawyer work on it. Make certain that the contents of the form are not in violation of the state Scaffolding Act.

- the release form should state that in consideration for the opportunity to work on the mural project, the signer is releasing the building owner and project director and sponsors from any responsibility in case of accident or injury incurred in any connection with the (_____) project, located at (_____), date (_____), under direction and sponsorship of (_____). Specify all aspects of the project.

20   Copyright

Though it has not often been done in the U.S., we recommend that you look into having your mural copyrighted. This is both a possible and a desirable step to take. Copyright is the right of an author, composer, or artist to control the reproduction of his or her work of art, and it protects the work from exploitation by commercial interests without the artist's permission.

Copyright restrains people other than the copyright owner from reproducing the original art work without the owner's consent. On the other hand, it does not hamper what is called "fair use" by others for legitimate purposes of study, research, criticism, and review. Thus the art work may be commented on and quoted, or reproduced for these purposes without permission.

To obtain copyright forms or other information, write to:

> The Registrar of Copyrights
> Copyright Office
> The Library of Congress
> Washington, D.C. 20025

They will send proper forms, on request, free of charge. (There is a $6.00 filing fee when the forms are sent in.) Fine arts intended solely for "ornamental purposes not generally susceptible of commercial reproduction" can be recorded by using the Copyright Office's Application Form G. Photographs can be used to document the work when filing.

The most important part of the copyright procedure is to put a copyright notice on the art work. It must be painted right on the mural by the date of dedication (in order to be valid) and should read:

> Copyright © [date] by [artist's or organization's name] *All Rights Reserved*

Be sure to include one photograph that clearly shows the copyright notice when filing.

We would note here that although art works can be copyrighted, names, titles, and slogans cannot be. Ideas do not qualify for copyright -- "it is the *expression* of an idea which qualifies."

The copyright law is constantly changing (and may, hopefully, change to further benefit the creative worker). If you have any questions, write to the Copyright Office or consult a copyright lawyer.

21 Helpful Hints

Here is a list of tips, shortcuts, warnings, and special materials that we've found useful (or wish we'd known about!) on our own mural projects or those of our friends.

MATERIALS

- *reducing lens*. A glass lens that reduces the size of an image. You can look through it to see how a mural that you're close to will look from a distance. It's useful if you are painting a portable mural in a small classroom or studio and don't have room to step back far enough to judge how it will look at a long distance. You can get a reducing lens in a camera store, optical store, or a large art supply store.

- *erasing sponge*. A dry sponge ("drycleaning sponge") that will quickly and easily erase chalk and charcoal lines from the wall or from a drawing. Get it at a hardware or paint store.

- *straight-edge board with handles*. Take a long, narrow board up to 6 or 8 feet long, and attach two kitchen cabinet handles to one side about 3' apart. Then you can hold it against the wall to guide yourself when you paint straight lines -- without painting on your fingers. Some artists have simply used a wooden slat from a venetian blind, finding it straight, light, and easy to handle. You can also use a yardstick.

- *mounted sketch*. When you're ready to work outside, mount your sketch on a piece of masonite panel or stiff cardboard. Then cover the sketch with a sheet of clear plastic. This will keep the sketch from crumpling or blowing around, and will protect it from paint drips. Leave one of the four edges of the plastic unattached so you can slip other detail drawings, photos, etc., into the clear folio.

- *snap line*. An extremely helpful gadget used for making straight lines on walls. It has a string coated with chalk that you can pull out, stretch tight against a wall, and snap to leave a chalk impression of a long, straight line. It's excellent for making grid lines on a wall, and it's inexpensive and easy to use. You can get it at a hardware or paint store.

- *color cards*. Color cards from a paint or art store can be used to get ideas for colors and to see how colors look next to each other.

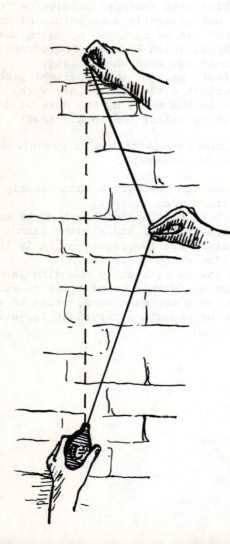

● *coffee cans and margarine tins.* Collect lots of these with lids to mix and store paints in. On a large wall, you might need 20-30 or more.

● *brushes.* On a smooth wall or on panels, good quality brushes are preferable. On rough walls, short, stiff bristle brushes are often best to paint with -- you may have to stab or jam the paint into holes in the brick or mortar.

   1. for latex or acrylic paints, nylon-bristle brushes (with "exploded" or frayed tips) are best.

   2. for oil-base paints, either nylon or natural bristles are fine, but natural bristles work better (though they're more expensive).

● *rollers.* Though paint rollers don't work especially well on brick walls, they are excellent (better than brushes, except in small areas) for use on rough concrete surfaces. They also work fine on wood or plaster walls.

● *paints.*

   1. always get paints of the same base, water or oil, etc. If you don't, they won't mix.

   2. try to get all paints of the same brand -- they will mix better, and color shades will be the same from batch to batch.

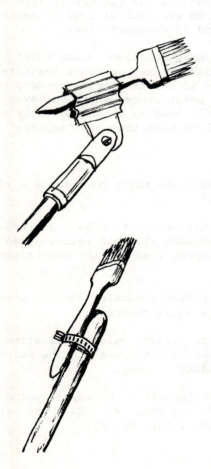

● *brush extender.* This is a gadget that allows you to attach your brush to a pole, to reach places you couldn't ordinarily reach. A brush extender can be adjusted so that you can change the angle of the brush. This is a good way to avoid taking risks on ladders and scaffolding. You can get a brush extender at some hardware stores and most paint stores.
   If you can't locate a brush extender, try jamming the end of your brush into a hollow aluminum tube. Or get a small clamp and clamp your brush to the pole.

● *shopping cart.* Try to borrow a shopping cart to carry paints and equipment to and from the mural site. Or get a kid's old wagon. This can really make a difference if you have any distance to travel.

● *ladder hooks.* These are extremely useful little devices if you are using ladders. They are simple hooks that attach to the handle of a paint can so that you can hang it on the rung of the ladder as you work.

THINGS TO DO

- get the landlord's permission, preferably in writing, before you do much work on the project. Some landlords insist on seeing a sketch before they will give permission.

- buy some cheap shirts and pants at Goodwill for your team to paint in. (If you know someone who does silkscreening, it's easy to decorate T-shirts for the team. This helps build spirit and is relatively cheap.)

- try to get a local hamburger place or restaurant to provide free lunches for the team.

- while you're painting, set the paints beside you on a box or small table. This saves continual bending over to dip your brush, which can be exhausting over a period of several hours.

- save leftover specially mixed colors (in coffee cans with lids) to use later on for touch-up and repair. You may not be able to mix the same color again.

- get help on documentation. Sometimes photo-documentation, taping, video-taping, etc., can be done by students from nearby colleges or high schools. Often students can get credit from the art, art history, or even social studies departments for this kind of documentation.

- Call in experts. Many questions about mural painting are complex or new, so don't hesitate to call on experts in related fields to help out. But be cautious: paint store owners, or even paint chemists, will tend to recommend their own products, so speak to more than one "expert."

  For example:

  contact muralists who might have faced similar problems.

  contact sign painters -- they have a tremendous amount of experience with big walls. Read the name of the company that did the advertisement and call up.

  when building portable murals, contact a set designer from a local theater.

  for questions on paints, paint application, and wall preparation, ask to speak to the paint chemist at a paint company.

  for reference materials -- books, clipping and photo files, films, etc. -- contact the head librarian of the local library.

Appendix

The U.S. Mural Movement

The current U.S. mural renaissance began in Chicago in 1967 with the "Wall of Respect," painted under the leadership of William Walker. And from that time on, it has been marked by tremendous enthusiasm on the part of both muralists and their audiences -- the people who live and work near the murals. Many recent U.S. murals express deep involvement with their communities, representing the aspirations and struggles of groups within neighborhoods, community centers, ethnic groups, unions, health centers, women's groups, teen-age gangs, and schools. They have not only drawn excitement from their immediate daily audiences, but have also received extensive newspaper and television coverage. They are the subject of a growing number of well-illustrated articles and books.

The projects are often organized by muralists in conjunction with community groups and leaders. Funding is sometimes from government or private foundations, but in most cases is the result of donations from the community or piecemeal fundraising by mural teams and local sponsors. In this way, as well as in their themes, the murals grow organically out of their communities and are a part of these communities' daily lives. Most murals are referred to with pride and are protected and respected by the community. Often they are used as rallying places for neighborhood activities, including meetings, demonstrations and celebrations.

Partly because of the lack of financial resources, contemporary mural painters have usually used relatively inexpensive house paints and bulletin colors in their murals. Often, because of the deterioration of buildings, murals have been done on walls that are decaying -- literally crumbling beneath the paint. Many important works are thus fading, are peeling, or are seriously threatened. In addition, the ravages of urban renewal and insensitive realtors have become a major enemy of current murals. Destruction of murals in this way, in fact, indicates in an inverted way the power of the murals -- that they represent a kind of consciousness that these interests do not like. Most recent U.S. murals are not "eternal" (and actually they make no pretense of "transcending the lives" of people). Outdoor murals have a projected life span that ranges at most to a decade or so under the best conditions.

Since the murals are among the most prominent examples of public art in the U.S., it seems to us that the standard used in judging them should be one that sees human interests as the major concern in art and wants to examine the ways in which artistic skills can help to serve the basic needs of people. Thus the central question to ask regarding a mural is how does it affect the people's lives -- does it advance human dignity? The best murals are allies of the people, giving strength in realizing their fullest human potential.

The most immediate context in which this judgment must be made is the community surrounding the mural; the mural should first be understood as it relates to the people and the issues of that community. But also in a more general way, murals are strong when they promote human dignity; when they combat racism and the exploitation of women within the context of whatever specific issue they're dealing with; when they show and celebrate human understanding. In all of this, the artistic skill of the muralist is best judged by its success in expressing and supporting these human interests.

Murals in ethnic communities are frequently distinguished by their thematic material, and often stress pride and communicate information about racial origins, histories, and traditions. In black and Latin neighborhoods, the overriding issue is the political awakening of the community. In black communities, for instance, Muhammed Ali and Martin Luther King, Jr., are the most frequently portrayed figures. Many black communities, such as Watts, have found superior artistic expression through such forms as dancing, theater, writing, and the like, but black muralists have been especially outstanding in giving leadership to the current mural movement. Latin communities can draw on the exceptionally rich tradition of public art and murals exemplified in the great Mexican walls. Their styles often reach further back, to pre-conquest Aztec symbols and a spectacular use of color, bold forms, and fierce mythical figures. Themes are often centered around the concept of Aztlan -- the Chicano territory -- geographical and spiritual -- within the U.S. and ethnic exploitation.

After beginning in the black community, and then having received leadership from both black and Latin communities, exciting murals have been done and continue to be done in many areas by a variety of groups. Among these are murals by Chinese, Japanese, and Native American groups, as well as by women's groups, neighborhood centers, unions, health clinics, and schools. Middle-class neighborhoods often have murals with surreal styles and subjects, cartoon characters, psychedelic, or fantasy themes. Business areas often exhibit geometrical designs and "super-graphics." Murals of this type are often distinguished by the professional or commercial nature of their styles, due to funds available for them. Schools are bringing in artists-in-residence to work with the students on subjects related to their studies and their lives in- and outside of school. Classroom and school murals, including mosaic, ceramic, and other types, as well as painted murals, have been done by all age groups and in schools throughout the country. There is also a growing use of "environmental" decoration in public and private buildings and on delivery vans, garbage trucks, water towers, etc.; these bring color and visual impact to their locations.

The current U.S. mural movement is growing in scope and importance. With it has grown the artistic presence of many groups denied other means of communicating to the society as a whole. These groups are now being heard and listened to with the help of the artworks that grow out of their communities. Their murals have as their main purpose not decoration or beautification of neighborhoods; they are not merely painted on walls, but speak of the walls, of the community, and its people, and demand justice and human dignity.

-- Tim Drescher

1930s Murals — The New Deal

In the 1930s, in the midst of the Great Depression, there was a major movement in the United States to "bring art back to the people" through murals in public buildings. Between 1933 and 1943, artists on government payrolls painted over 4,000 murals. Many of these murals have survived to this day and remain, almost unnoticed, on the walls of post offices, schools, libraries, and other public buildings. They show the optimism and determination of their era, in contrast to the terrible economic realities during which they were created.

Throughout the 1930s, the major political and social issue facing the country was unemployment. Millions of people could not find jobs, so the government created some. Roosevelt's New Deal administration established a number of public works programs which provided the unemployed with work instead of relief handouts, and at the same time made physical and artistic improvements throughout the country. Under the authority of the Civilian Conservation Corps (CCC), the Public Works Administration (PWA), the National Youth Administration (NYA), and the Works Progress Administration (WPA), armies of workers spread out across the country digging ditches, building highways and mountain trails, planting forests, laying sidewalks, constructing public buildings, and painting murals.

Thus the federal government became an art patron. In spite of administrative complexities, much exceptional work was accomplished. Works of art were commissioned under four separate programs. Three of these were run by the Department of the Treasury, which sponsored murals in such government buildings as post offices and courthouses. The largest and most creative program, however, was the WPA's Federal Art Project. It provided murals for tax-supported institutions, such as schools, hospitals, prisons, and airports. At its peak, it provided over 5,000 artists with steady jobs. The WPA maintained a permanent corps of artists in each state who worked five days a week for reasonable wages. They created not only murals, but also did easel paintings, prints, sculptures, posters, bas reliefs, museum dioramas, textiles, parade floats -- whatever the community needed in the way of art work.

Soon art works in public places were not unusual. Traveling exhibitions visited small towns, and WPA community art centers offered lessons to all comers. The Index of American Design sought out and recorded native crafts like quilting, doll making, and sign painting. Other WPA cultural projects began at the same time: The Federal Theater Project, Federal Writer's Project, and the Federal Music Project. Photographers and filmmakers went to work for the Farm Security Administration. Although the Depression was a traumatic time in America, it was also a time of great artistic achievement.

Among these cultural programs, the murals stood out particularly. Complaints about the New Deal art policies, about "giving" money to "lazy bohemians," were answered with references to the murals. They could be defended as public, useful, and instructive -- the result of cooperative efforts, and a "lot of art for the money." Most impressive, the artists worked at the request of the public, not just on their own. Any tax-supported institution could commission a mural from its state WPA Art Project, and had to pay only for canvas, paint, and other supplies; the labor and artistic skills were provided through the government. The murals which resulted were collaborations between the artist, his or her assistants, the state's project administrators, and the "client" -- usually a school principal, municipal librarian, or prison warden.

About 80 percent of the murals created in this period were done in oil paint on canvas, although other media such as egg tempera, casein, mosaic and fresco were also used. The murals were usually painted at the state's art project headquarters and than transported to the sponsoring institution and attached to the proper wall.

In subject and style, the murals differed widely. Although there was some censorship of content (forbidden, for example, were nudity, political caricature, and religious symbolism), muralists had a great deal of freedom. Topics ranged from "Assimilation of the Immigrant into the Industrial Life of Madison, Illinois," and "Characters from Hans Christian Andersen," to "The Growth of Medicine from Primitive Times" and "Louis Sullivan." Stylistically, the influence of the Mexican muralists who worked at various times in the United States during this period was felt, but was not dominant. In fact, for a government-sponsored program, the stylistic and thematic diversity is remarkable. Many totally abstract murals were done in New York City under the WPA.

Murals still stand as one of the best examples of the New Deal philosophy of art. This was a time when art was declared to be a state resource to be harnessed for the public good, and when artists were determined to be no different from other workers. Artists were able to work as they wished, and were enabled to continue being artists without starving. Their mission was to "decorate" public places and bring art to the people. While there may be criticism of the subject matter of some murals, their vitality is undeniable. The project led to a flowering of the arts in America and provided a training ground for many later-prominent artists.

-- Barbara Bernstein

The Mexican Mural Movement

The 20th-century mural movement of Mexico, which has represented decades of socially oriented public art, shows dramatically the successful integration of political and aesthetic concerns. It is this movement to which the current U.S. mural movement looks for its greatest inspiration. The civil war in Mexico (1910-17), in which some of the leading Mexican muralists (like Siqueiros) fought, provided the impetus for the first surge of nationalistic murals. These murals were painted on the walls of the National Preparatory School in Mexico City during the early 1920s. They were intended to speak forcefully and directly to the largely illiterate people of Mexico. The artists involved in this early production (among them: David Siqueiros, 1896-1974; Diego Rivera, 1886-1957; José Clemente Orozco, 1886-1949; and Xavier Guerrero, 1896-   ) considered themselves workers for the Mexican revolution and formed a union -- the Union of Painters, Sculptors, and Technical Workers -- in 1923. In their manifesto, issued the same year, they renounced easel painting, which they viewed as an expression of the aristocratic class. They specifically called for the creation of monumental public art. They also called for renewed interest in, and exaltation of, the Mexican artistic tradition, especially the art of pre-conquest Mexico. Their themes dealt with the events of Mexican history before and during the Mexican revolution, and with the aspirations of the people for the future. While the federal government and private patrons were among their first and major sponsors, in the 1930s the trade unions also supported the movement.

The pronounced political swing to the right that occurred in Mexico during the late '20s and early '30s (personified by the most powerful political figure of the period, Plutarco Elias Calles) had dire consequences, temporarily, for the muralists' artistic production. During the '30s Orozco, Rivera, and Siqueiros worked in the United States, where their art had great impact upon socially involved North American artists then working on the New Deal projects, including Anton Refregier, Ben Shahn, William Gropper, and Phillip Evergood. Following the election in Mexico of Lázaro Cárdenas (1934-40), the "second wave" of the mural movement began. This period was especially fruitful for Orozco, who produced his masterworks in Guadalajara and Jilquilpan (Cárdenas's home town) during this period. With the death of Orozco in 1949 and Rivera in 1957, Siqueiros alone of the "Tres Grandes" continued to work in the expression of political public art until his recent death in 1974.

The murals of the Mexicans have received scant attention in this country since the 1930s. This speaks not only for the lack of interest in 20th-century Latin American art on the part of North American critics and historians, but also for the turning away from social issues in the art produced in the U.S. during the Cold War period. Yet there are signs that there may be renewed interest growing in this country

about Latin American art. Recent interest in the New
Deal period (see "Bibliography"), has led people to
look again at murals done during the Depression. The
development of political awareness, especially in the
black and Latin communities of the United States, has
led artists of these communities to find visual expression through the production of murals in their
neighborhoods. As communities begin to seek knowledge
of their histories and to express their traditions,
culture, and hopes, their artists will look toward
the Mexican muralists for inspiration.

The current mural renaissance in the United States
has learned much from the Mexican murals, but there
is still a great deal more investigation needed con-
cerning these artists' history and techniques of
painting, and about the murals themselves. The more
we study this great movement, the more our own public
artworks will benefit.

-- Larry Hurlburt

Bibliography

We are including this bibliography for those who want to look further at murals and mural techniques. Some of these books are available for sale; others are located in most large public libraries. This bibliography is concerned mainly with 20th-century murals, and is divided into four sections: Techniques, Recent U.S. Murals, New Deal (WPA) Period, and the Mexican Mural Movement.

Both the Mexican and New Deal artists produced very important public works of art. Even so, art historians have largely ignored both groups. Recently, however, the New Deal period has finally begun to receive the attention it deserves. Hopefully, the Mexican muralists will soon begin to get the same attention.

TECHNIQUES

Cennini, Cennino d'Andrea, *The Craftsman's Handbook (Il Libro dell' Arte)*, (New York: Dover paperback, 1954).

One of the most influential technical manuals ever written, this 15th-century Florentine account was the "textbook" of the Mexicans in the 1920s.

Mayer, Ralph, *The Artists Handbook of Materials and Techniques* (New York, Viking Press, 1970).

Comprehensive account of variety and permanence of painting and sculpture materials. Chapter on murals.

Doerner, Max, *Materials of the Artist* (New York: Harcourt Brace and Co., 1934).

Academic survey of artists' technique in more traditional terminology.

Kay, Reed, *The Painter's Companion* (Cambridge: Webb Books, Inc., 1963).

A basic guide to technical problems for the artist. Deals with paint application, paint chemistry, and other artist's materials.

Gutierrez, José, *From Fresco to Plastics: New Materials for Easel and Mural Paintings* (Ottowa: National Gallery of Canada, 1952).

Gutierrez, José, *Painting with Acrylics* (New York: Watson-Guptill Publications, 1969).

These are two very important works by the mural technician of the Mexican movement, who founded (with D. A. Siqueiros) in 1945 a mural workshop to explore techniques at the National Polytechnic

Institute in Mexico City. Both books have introductions by Siqueiros.

Hale, Gardner, *Fresco Painting* (New York: Dover paperback, 1970).

Preface by J. C. Orozco.

Nelson, Glenn C., *A Potter's Handbook*, 2nd edition (New York: Holt, Rinehart and Winston, 1966).

Contains information on uses of clay in older cultures and contemporary forms; mentions architectural ceramics. Well illustrated with technical information for different levels of experience.

Rhodes, Daniel, *Clay and Glazes for the Potter* (Philadelphia: Chilton, 1957).

Technical information for ceramic projects.

Rosenberg, Lilli Ann Killen, Ken Wittenberg, Photographer, *Children Make Murals and Sculpture* (New York: Reinhold Book Corp., 1968).

Beautiful color photos of classroom and community art projects in different media -- very inspirational.

Randall, Arne, *Murals for Schools -- Sharing Creative Experiences* (Worcester, Mass.: Davis Press, Inc., 1956).

Different classroom projects, mainly murals painted on paper.

Further Adventures of Cardboard Carpentry, published in 1972 by Workshop for Learning Things, Inc., 5 Bridge Street, Watertown, Mass. 02172.

Covers simple triwall design from room dividers to domes; published by a company which makes very useful tools for triwall carpentry (circle cutters, dowel threaders, slot cutters, etc.).

RECENT U.S. MURALS AND RELATED MATERIAL

Cry for Justice, published by the Amalgamated Meat Cutters and Butcher Workmen of North America, Chicago, 1972. 22 pages. (Available through Public Art Workshop.)

Excellent commentary and numerous color illustrations on the contemporary mural movement in Chicago.

Garcia, Rupert, *Raza Murals and Muralists: An Historical View*, San Francisco, 1974. 35 pages. (Available through Public Art Workshop.)

From Pre-Hispanic murals through the 20th-century murals in Mexico to the recent Chicano murals in the U.S., concentrating in San Francisco. Includes photos.

Rubin, Sandy, and Bob Rivera, *A Primer for Community Graffiti Workshops*, Center for Alternative Graffiti Workshop, Philadelphia, 1972. 24 pages. (Available through Public Art Workshop.)

Ideas for community group projects and the setting up of graffiti alternative workshops. Includes photos.

"The Chicago Muralists," *American Dialog*, Vol. 7, No. 2, 1972, pp. 23-25. (Reprint available through Public Art Workshop.)

An article written by leading Chicago muralists for the "Murals for the People" exhibit at the Museum of Contemporary Art, Chicago. Includes photos.

Bloom, Janet, "Changing Walls," *The Architectural Forum,* Vol. 138, No. 4, May 1973, pp. 20-27. (Reprint available through Public Art Workshop.)

Excellent article giving a glance at murals, muralists, and mural centers around the U.S. Includes color photos.

Kroll, Eric, "Folk Art in the Barrios," *Natural History*, Vol. LXXXII, No. 5, May 1973, pp. 56-65. (Reprint available through Public Art Workshop.)

Excellent article featuring the murals of Santa Fe by Chicano artists. Includes excellent color photos.

Patlan, Ray, and John Weber, "A Wall Belongs to Everybody," *Youth Magazine*, September 1972, pp. 58-66. United Church Press, 1505 Race Street, Philadelphia.

Experiences of the community mural painters and their teams. Includes color photos.

Weber, John, "Murals as People's Art," *Liberation*, Vol. 16, No. 4, 1971, 339 Lafayette Street, New York, 10012.

A theoretical discussion and observations based on experience with the recent Chicago murals. Includes photos.

Cockcroft, Eva A., and James D., "Murals for the People of Chile," *TRA*, No. 4, 1973. (Reprint available through Public Art Workshop.)

Article with photos on the history and functioning of Brigada Ramona Para Mural Movement which flowered under the Popular Unity government of Chile.

Charlot, Jean, *The Charlot Murals in Georgia* (Athens: University of Georgia Press, 1941). (Reprint of first chapter available through Public Art Workshop.)

First chapter contains an excellent article entitled "Public Speaking in Paint" by an artist deeply involved with the Mexican Mural Movement.

Refregier, Anton, "Governmental Sponsorship of the Arts," reprinted from *Public Ownership in the U.S.A.*, New York, 1961. 10 pages. (Reprint available through Public Art Workshop.)

Describes the necessity for government sponsorship and support of the arts.

THE NEW DEAL PERIOD

Aaron, D., and R. Bendimer, eds., *The Strenuous Decade: A Social and Intellectual Record of the 1930's* (New York: Anchor paperback, 1970).

Selected articles representing different points of view from the '30s, with bibliography.

Contreras, Belisario R., *Treasury Art Programs: The New Deal and the American Artist, 1933 to 1943*, unpublished Ph.D. dissertation, American University, 1967. (Available through University Microfilms, Ann Arbor, Michigan.)

An in-depth study of Public Works of Art Project, Treasury Section of Painting and Sculpture, and the Treasury Relief Project.

North, Joseph, *New Masses: An Anthology of the Rebel Thirties* (New York: International Publishers, 1969).

Selection of writings from a prominent labor and left cultural magazine of the '30s.

O'Connor, Francis V., "New Deal Murals in New York," *Artforum*, November 1968, pp. 41-49.

O'Connor, Francis V., *Federal Support for the Visual Arts: The New Deal and Now* (Greenwich, Conn.: The New York Graphic Society, 1969).

Comprehensive bibliography on New Deal art from the 1930s to the present (1969).

O'Connor, Francis V., *The New Deal Art Projects: An Anthology of Memoirs*. Washington, D.C.: Smithsonian Institution, 1972).

O'Connor, Francis V., *Art for the Millions* (Greenwich, Conn.: New York Graphic Society, 1973).

Sixty-seven essays by WPA artists and administrators written during the 1930s, but never before published.

THE MEXICAN MURAL MOVEMENT

This section is organized as follows: first are the surveys and more general works; then follow writings on "the three greats" of the movement -- Rivera, Siqueiros, and Orozco.

Charlot, Jean, *The Mexican Mural Renaissance, 1920-25* (New Haven: Yale University Press, 1963).

Account of the first years of the movement by one of its founders.

Meyers, Bernard, *Mexican Painting in Our Time* (New York: Oxford University Press, 1956).

Probably the best of the books dealing in general with the Mexican movement; still leaves much to be desired, however.

Rodriguez, Antonio, *A History of Mexican Mural Painting* (New York: G.P. Putnam's Sons, 1969).

From pre-conquest times to the present. The most recent of the surveys; good illustrations.

Reed, Alma *The Mexican Muralists* (New York: Crown Publishers, 1960).

A brief survey with photos of many artists.

Mural Painting of the Mexican Revolution, 1921-1960; published in 1960 by The Editorial Fund for Mexican Plastic Arts, Banco Nacional de Comercio Exterior, S.A., Venustiano Carranza, Num. 32, Mexico, D.F.

A large volume of excellent quality color and black and white photos of the great Mexican murals.

Plenn, Jaime, and Virginia, *A Guide to Modern Mexican Murals* (Mexico; Ediciones Tolteca, 1963). (Map available through Public Art Workshop.)

Extremely useful for locating the major murals in Mexico City; includes "coded" maps of murals there. Also lists murals outside of Mexico.

Suarez, Orlando, *Inventario del Muralismo Mexicano: Siglo VII a. de c., 1968*, UNAM, 1972.

Definitive listing of 20th-century Mexican artists and murals. Not only updates Plenn book, but greatly surpasses it in range of coverage.

Brenner, Anita, *The Wind that Swept Mexico, 1910-42* (New York: Harper, 1943).

Interesting photographic history of Mexico during the most important period of the mural movement.

Robinson, Ione, *A Wall to Paint On* (New York: E.P. Dutton and Co., 1946).

Wordy, though interesting, account by a North American painter who worked in Mexico during the 1920s and 1930s.

Rivera

Evans, Ernestine, *The Frescoes of Diego Rivera* (New York: Harcourt, Brace and Co., 1929).

Excellent photographs of Rivera's work through the National Agricultural School, Chapingo (his most important work).

Diego Rivera: 50 Años de su Labor Artistica, Institute Nacional de Bellas Artes, Mexico, 1951.

The most complete one-volume work on Rivera; essays and many photographs.

Rivera, Diego (with Bertram D. Wolfe), *Portrait of America* (New York: Covici-Friede, 1934).

Photographs of Rivera's North American murals, with United States "history" by Wolfe and Rivera.

Wolfe, Bertram D., *The Fabulous Life of Diego Rivera* (New York: Stein & Day, 1963).

Enthusiastic and uncritical account of Rivera by a fervent North American admirer.

Kozloff, Max, "The Rivera Frescoes of Modern Industry at the Detroit Institute of Arts: Proletarian Art under Capitalist Patronage," *Artforum*, November 1973.

Sympathetic view of Rivera's 1932 Detroit project by an important Younger U.S. critic.

Siqueiros

Siqueiros: Through the Road of a Neo-Realism or Modern Social Painting in Mexico, Instituto Nacional de Bellas Artes, Mexico, 1951.

Trilingual (English, French, and Spanish) publication of importance; 215 photographs of Siqueiros's work to 1951, along with comments by Siqueiros on his art.

Micheli, Mario de, *Siqueiros* (New York: Abrams, 1968).

    A typical Abrams production: expensive, little text, but with good photographs.

Tibol, Raquel, *David Alfaro Siqueiros* (Mexico: Empresas Editoriales, 1961).

    Contains many important documents pertinent to Siqueiros's career.

Tibol, Raquel, *Siqueiros: Introductor de Realidades*, Universidad Nacional Autonomo de Mexico, 1961.

    Account of Siqueiros by his Mexican biographer.

Orozco

Fernandez, Justino, *José Clemente Orozco: Forma e Idea,* Universidad de Mexico, Instituto de Investigaciones Esteticas, 1942.

    A basic study of Orozco by the foremost contemporary Mexican art historian.

Helm, McKinley, *Man of Fire: J.C. Orozco* (New York: Harcourt, Brace and Co., 1953).

    Written by a North American acquaintance of Orozco four years after Orozco's death.

Orozco, J.C., *Textos de Orozco*, ed. Justino Fernandez, Universidad Nacional Autonomo de Mexico, Instituto de Investigaciones Esteticas, 1955.

Orozco, J.C., *An Autobiography* (Austin: University of Texas Press, 1962).

    Brief and to the point; ends in 1936 as Orozco began his masterworks in Guadalajara.

Reed, Alma, *José Clemente Orozco* (New York: Delphic Studios, 1932).

    Excellent photographs of Orozco's work up to his Dartmouth Murals.

Reed, Alma, *Orozco* (New York: Oxford University Press, 1956).

    A valuable account, primarily of Orozco's North American period, 1927-34, by a person who knew him well.

Scott, David W., "Orozco's Prometheus," *College Art Journal*, XVII, No. 1 (Fall 1951).

    The only serious study by a North American art historian on any of the Mexican's work in this country. This article concerns Orozco's Prometheus fresco at Pomona College, Claremont, California.

Photo Identification

CHAPTER 1: 1. "Under City Stone," Caryl Yasko, director, Chicago (photo by Public Art Workshop).

CHAPTER 2: 2. Detail, "Under City Stone"; 3. "La Destrucción del Mono Blanco," Casa Aztlan, Ray Patlan, director, Chicago (photo by Sim Der); 4. "Resurrection," St. Dominick's Church, Keithen Carter, director, Chicago (photo by Public Art Workshop); 5. Bank of America, Jesus Campusano, San Francisco (photo by Tim Drescher); 6. Detail of Bank of America; 7. Chapel mural, Archdiocesan Latin American Committee, Lillian Brulc, Chicago (photo by RE:SOURCE); 8. San Diego-Coronado bridge support, Group de Santana Artists, San Diego (photo by John Bright); 9. "Anti-Drug Abuse Mural," Al Smith Recreation Center, Susan Shapiro-Kiok, director, New York (photo by Alan Okada); 10. Bus bench, Jesus Gutierrez, Los Angeles (photo by John Bright); 11. "Mi Abuelita," Judy Baca, director, Los Angeles (photo by L.A. Dept. of Recreation and Parks); 12. "Oh Speak, Speak," James Woods, director, Watts, Los Angeles (photo by John Bright); 13, 14, 15, 16, and 17 (photos by Public Art Workshop).

CHAPTER 3: 18. (photo by Public Art Workshop).

CHAPTER 4: 19. (photo by Public Art Workshop).

CHAPTER 5: 20. "All of Mankind," Saint Marcello Church, William Walker, Chicago (photo by Public Art Workshop); 21. "Break the Grip of the Absentee Landlord," Mark Rogovin, director, Chicago (photo by Public Art Workshop); 22. "The Third Nail," James Brown, Roxbury, Mass. (photo by Pam Peterson); 23. "Sunburst," Iron Men of the 5th City Community, Chicago (photo by Sim Der); 24. "Save the Chinatown Church," Don Kaiser, Sharon Loe, Philadelphia (photo by Patrick Radebaugh); 25. "Liberty and Education," Artes Guadalupanos de Aztlan, Santa Fe, N.M. (photo by Artes Guadalupanos de Aztlan); 26. Detail, "Our Government Has Destroyed, Our People Must Rebuild" (portable mural), Public Art Workshop, East Berlin, G.D.R. (photo by Public Art Workshop); 27. "Child Care Is Our Right--Cuidado Para Ninos Es Nuestro Derecho," Washington Heights Child Care Center, Washington Heights Child Care Team, New York (photo by Peter Bower); 28. Detail, "Child Care Is Our Right . . . ; 29. "Wall of Respect," William Walker, Eugene Eda, and members of OBAC, Chicago (photo by RE:SOURCE); 30. Detail, "Wall of Respect"; 31. Detail, "Wall of Respect" (photo by Sim Der); 32. Detail in progress, "History of Struggle in Pennsylvania," Thomas Nabried Center, Toni Truesdale, director, Philadelphia (photo by Milton Rogovin); 33. "The Crucifixion of Don Pedro Albizu Campos," Puerto Rican Art Association, Chicago (photo by Public Art Workshop); 34. "Arise from Oppression, Henry Street Settlement Playhouse, Susan Caruso-Green, James Januzzi, directors, New York (photo by Alan Okada).

CHAPTER 6: 35. Detail, "Break the Grip of the Absentee Landlord," Mark Rogovin, director, Chicago (photo by Public Art Workshop); 36. "Protect the Peoples' Homes," Mark Rogovin, director, Chicago (photo by Sim Der); 37. "Peace and Salvation, Wall of Understanding," William Walker, Chicago (photo by Public Art Workshop); 38. Detail, "Peace and Salvation"; 39. Detail, "Wall of Brotherhood," Universal Savings and Loan Association, Mario Castillo, Chicago (photo by Sim Der); 40. Detail, "I.O.U.," Holly Highfill, director, Chicago (photo by Public Art Workshop); 41. "Let a People Loving Freedom, Come to Growth," Wright Brothers School, Lucy Mahler, director, New York (photo by Terry Santana); 42. Detail, "400 Years of Struggle," W.E.B. Du Bois Community Center, Lucy Mahler, director, New York (photo by Dave Dubnau).

43. Detail, "Jamestown Mural," Consuelo Mendez, San Francisco (photo by Fred Gonzalez);44. Detail, "Hay Cultura en Nuestra Comunidad," Casa Aztlan, Ray Patlan, director, Chicago (photo by Ray Patlan); 45. Detail, "Wall of Meditation," Olivet Presbyterian Church, Eugene Eda, Chicago (photo by Sim Der); 46. Detail in progress, "Rip Off," Mitchell Caton, director, Chicago (photo by Public Art Workshop); 47. Detail, "Black Man's Dilemma," Don McIlvaine, director, Chicago (photo by Sim Der); 48. Detail, "Nation Time," Mitchell Caton, Chicago (Public Art Workshop); 49. Sketch, "Wall of Brotherhood," Universal Savings and Loan Assocation, Mario Castillo, director, Chicago (photo by Harold Allen); 50. "Wall of Brotherhood"; 51. "Plumed Serpent," Willie Herron, Los Angeles (photo by John Bright); 52. "Peoples' Handshake," Chicago Fine Arts Guild, Chicago (photo by Public Art Workshop); 53. Construction fence, Hamilton, Ontario, Canada (photo by Public Art Workshop); 54. Detail, "Rio Mapocho Mural," Brigada Ramona Para, Santiago, Chile(photo by Lucy Mahler).

CHAPTER 7: 55. Mural in progress, Astrid Fuller, Chicago (photo by Public Art Workshop); 56. (photo by Public Art Workshop); 57. Sketch, "Unity of the People," Mark Rogovin, director, Chicago (photo by Public Art Workshop); 58, 59. Details in progress, "Unity of the People."

CHAPTER 10: 60. (photo by Ray Patlan); 61. Detail, school building, Donetzk, U.S.S.R. (photo by Public Art Workshop); 62. Detail, "Our Neighborhood," Alvarado School, Nancy Thompson, director, San Francisco (photo by Tim Drescher); 63. (photo by Ken Wittenberg, Children Make Murals and Sculpture); 64. In progress, "The Beginning," First Unitarian Church, Kathy Judge and students, Chicago (photo by Nancy Hays); 65. In progress, "The Beginning" (photo by Nancy Hays); 66. Detail, "The Beginning" (photo by Public Art Workshop); 67.Detail in progress, "Toward Freedom," Columbia College, Mark Rogovin, director, Chicago (photo by Public Art Workshop); 68. (photo by Public Art Workshop); 69. (photo by Ken Wittenberg, Children Make Murals and Sculpture); 70. Untitled, A. A. Stagg High School, Deeks Carroll and students, Palos Hills, Illinois (photo by Deeks Carroll); 71. In progress (photo by Deeks Carroll); 72. (photo by Deeks Carroll).

CHAPTER 11: 73. "Vote Your Future" (portable mural), Public Art Workshop, Chicago (photo by Public Art Workshop); 74. Detail, "Vote Your Future"; 75. In progress, "Bored of Education," St. Mary's Center for Learning, Marie Burton and students, Chicago (photo by Bob Natkin); 76. "Bored of Education" (photo by Marie Burton); 77. "Bored of Education" (photo by Marie Burton); 78. "Bored of Education" (photo by Bob Natkin).

CHAPTER 14: 79. Blank wall, "Break the Grip of the Absentee Landlord," Mark Rogovin, director, Chicago (photo by Public Art Workshop); 80. In progress, "Break the Grip of the Absentee Landlord"; 81, 82, 83. "Break the Grip of the Absentee Landlord"; 84. Detail, "Break the Grip of the Absentee Landlord."

CHAPTER 15: 85. "For the New World," Parish of the Holy Covenant, John Weber. Oscar Martinez, directors, Chicago (photo by Bob Natkin); 86. "Let a People Loving Freedom, Come to Growth," Lucy Mahler, director, New York (photo by Dave Dubnau); 87. "The Philosophy of the Spiritual," Mitchell Caton, Chicago (photo by Ted Lacey); 88. "Protect the Peoples' Homes," Mark Rogovin, director, Chicago (photo by Barry Burlison).

CHAPTER 18: 89. In progress, "Unity of the People," Mark Rogovin, director, Chicago (photo by Public Art Workshop); 90, 91, 92. (photos by Public Art Workshop).